Y0-BYL-775

Women in America

FROM COLONIAL TIMES TO THE 20TH CENTURY

Women in America

FROM COLONIAL TIMES TO THE 20TH CENTURY

Advisory Editors
LEON STEIN
ANNETTE K. BAXTER

A Note About This Volume

For Mary Edwards Walker (1832-1919) the world was out of joint. She became a doctor when the world wanted no women doctors. She considered women's clothes to be unhealthy and ridiculous and defiantly wore the Bloomer when most women preferred the bustle, but she denigrated professional women reformers and suffragists. In the Civil War she served in the Virginia and Tennessee battle zones and was captured. She received the Congressional Medal of Honor in 1865, but Congress withdrew it in 1917. Through it all she remained uncompromising in her convictions and continued to wear the kind of trousers she first donned in the army, later adding jackets, shirts, ties. In time she became an annoyance to some, a crank to others. But in *The Part Taken by Women in American History* (Arno Press, 1972), Mrs. John A. Logan writes of her, "Because of her determination to wear male attire, Dr. Walker has been made the subject of abuse and ridicule by people of narrow minds. It should be remembered that she is the only woman in the world who was an assistant army surgeon. She went to the front and served the Union army in a way that in any other country could have caused her to be recognized as a heroine of the nation. She draws a pension of exactly eight dollars and fifty cents a month, a half pension of her rank, in spite of the fact that she really deserves the highest recognition of the Government and the public."

DR. MARY WALKER

The Little Lady in Pants

CHARLES McCOOL SNYDER

ARNO PRESS
A New York Times Company
NEW YORK – 1974

Reprint Edition 1974 by Arno Press Inc.

Copyright © 1962, by Charles McCool Snyder
Reprinted by permission of Charles McCool Snyder

WOMEN IN AMERICA
From Colonial Times to the 20th Century
ISBN for complete set: 0-405-06070-X
See last pages of this volume for titles.

Manufactured in the United States of America

———◆———

Library of Congress Cataloging in Publication Data

Snyder, Charles McCool.
    Dr. Mary Walker.

    (Women in America: from colonial times to the
20th century)
    Reprint of the ed. published by Vantage Press, New
York.
    1. Walker, Mary Edwards, 1832-1919. I. Series.
R154.W18S5 1974   610'.92'4 [B]   74-3973
ISBN 0-405-06122-6

DR. MARY WALKER

The Little Lady in Pants

Dr. Mary Walker
This photograph of Dr. Walker, in her Army uniform, was taken just after the Civil War, when she was 33 years old. (Original in National Archives)

DR. MARY WALKER

The Little Lady in Pants

by

CHARLES McCOOL SNYDER

VANTAGE PRESS

NEW YORK   WASHINGTON   HOLLYWOOD

FIRST EDITION

*All rights reserved, including the right of
reproduction in whole or in part in any form*

Copyright, 1962, by Charles McCool Snyder

Published by Vantage Press, Inc.
120 West 31st Street, New York 1, N. Y.

Manufactured in the United States of America

PREFACE

I am indebted to a host of Oswegonians for their reminiscences of Dr. Mary Walker. Once I had launched my inquiry, they came in a flood: from the old Walker neighborhood in Oswego Town, on the street corners, and through the mail and over the phone.

I would single out for special mention the recollections of Fred Haynes, who has lived across the road from the Walker homestead for seventy years, Mildred Candee and Helen Quigley, grandnieces of Dr. Walker, and Mrs. Isabelle Kingsbury Hart and Dr. Joseph Ringland of Oswego.

Reina Gardner Hamilton of State College, Pennsylvania, a descendant of Belva Lockwood, and Julia Hull Winner of Lockport, New York, were helpful in establishing Dr. Walker's relations with Mrs. Lockwood. Mrs. M. C. Wheelwright of Des Moines assisted in reconstructing Dr. Walker's year in Iowa.

I would mention, also, Charlotte Story Perkinson of Norfolk, Virginia, who remembers from her childhood in New Hampshire an unexpected visit from Dr. Walker in quest of evidence in the Worden murder case. Dorothy Mozley of Springfield guided me to family materials in Massachusetts, and Jane F. Smith to manuscripts in the National Archives.

I am indebted to Mrs. Lillian Heagerty of Oswego and Newburgh for the preservation of the diary of Aurora B. Coats, with its insights into the Walker family life. In Middletown, New York, Mildred Parker Seese and Josephine Labow assisted in locating materials relating to Dr. Lydia Sayer Hasbrouck, a friend and fellow dress reformer of Dr. Walker. Miss Ida J. Draeger and her staff at the library of the Woman's Medical College of Pennsylvania were especially helpful, as were Mr. and Mrs. Richard Wright at the Onondaga Historical Society in Syracuse, Juanita Kersey and her associates at the Oswego Public Library, and Helen Hagger and her staff at the State University of New York, College of Education at Oswego.

Fred Wright, a local historian of Oswego, proved to be a storehouse of information on the Walkers and local traditions.

I would like to offer especial commendation to the persons responsible for the preservation of the Walker manuscripts. Thirty years ago the late Lida (Mrs. Charles W. W.) Poynter of Omaha, Nebraska, undertook a study of Dr. Walker, in the course of which she transcribed hundreds of pages of notes from family records then in the home of a nephew of Dr. Walker in Oswego Town. Years later Mrs. Eric Lawson of Canastota, N.Y., acquired a collection of Walker papers, which she presented to the Syracuse University Library. She also wrote an interesting paper on Dr. Walker, which is on deposit in the Syracuse University Library. Mrs. Charles Sivers of Oswego discovered a cache of Walker manuscripts at a local auction, and rescued them from oblivion.

The Oswego County Historical Society supplied a variety of Walker materials, including manuscripts, pictures and the Congressional Medal of Honor.

I am grateful to the Research Foundation of the State University of New York for a grant-in-aid, which permitted me to expand the scope of my study.

CONTENTS

Chapter I

SHE WOULD BE A PHYSICIAN

The stained pages of a faded diary reveal that its author was moving down the Ohio River on a steamboat, a recent innovation in these parts. The date was April 9, 1820, and the boat was approaching Louisville.[1]

More than three years had elapsed since Alvah Walker, a native of Greenwich, Massachusetts, had gone West at nineteen. He had traveled by way of New York State, and presumably the Allegheny River to Pittsburgh, working as a carpenter in the river ports. The pause from his labors gave him time to reflect upon his youth: The death of his father "while sinking a stone";[2] leaving school at thirteen and being apprenticed to a carpenter in order to help support his mother and his seven younger sisters and brothers; his mother's remarriage, freeing him to strike out on his own.

He also found himself taking stock of his travels and pondering upon his future. He would work his way to New Orleans, where he would take passage for Boston. It was about time to settle down.

He spent a few weeks each in Louisville, Natchez, and New Orleans, earning his living by framing, hewing, and shingling. He viewed slavery on a cotton plantation, played roulette in Natchez-under-the-Hill, feasted on oranges, artichokes, and other Southern specialties, and heard alligators "bellow like bulls" in the swamps. He visited the battlefield near New Orleans where Jackson had slaughtered the Redcoats six years before, and saw the marks of cannon balls on the trees, and men's bones lying on the ground. He also observed myrtle trees "that looked like stacks of hay," and bay trees which remained green through the entire year. In fact, his roving eye missed little of the life of the old Mississippi.

At New Orleans he bought a mosquito bar, a supply of oranges, segars, and brandy, and a passage for Boston on the brig *Oliver*.

9

In the gulf he witnessed porpoises which "blow like a man blowing away mosquitoes," and diverted himself with the other passengers drinking rum and eggnog, playing cards and checkers, in which he excelled, fishing and singing psalms. He slept in a sail basket, which swung like a hammock.

After a voyage of four weeks he set foot on the center wharf at Boston. A few blocks farther he sighted an old acquaintance. It was a startling experience after a four years' absence.

When the twenty-three-year-old wanderer reached home he was dined and wined by his numerous relatives (the Walkers were a seventeenth-century New England family), enjoyed the relaxation of fishing and swimming, gathered lilies in the neighboring ponds, and in the evenings joined friends in the proverbial quilting parties. When he viewed the Connecticut River, "it looked not half as large as it used to."

Now, with his feet on the ground, he decided to marry, and return to Kentucky. It took him just three months to find his mate: "Got my name made public with Vesta Whitcomb's, which surprised many sons and daughters of Adam" (he confided in his diary), and to complete preparations for the trip. He invested a small inheritance from his grandfather, obtained $79 in silver, bought a horse and wagon, and fashioned hoops to hold on a cover. He then joined hands in matrimony with the twenty-year-old Miss Whitcomb. The newlyweds departed the following morning for the West.

Little is known of Vesta Whitcomb, except that like her husband she had a long line of New England ancestors, including participants in both the French and Indian War and the American Revolution. She was also a cousin of Robert Ingersoll, famous nineteenth century orator, philosopher, and agnostic.

They drove steadily westward, averaging about thirty miles a day, and crossed the Hudson River on the fourth day. At Albany they took the Great Western Turnpike (New York Route 20 today), and after a week reached Otisco, near Syracuse, where they stopped with Vesta's sister, Sally Whitcomb Furniss. Two days later they rested again with Uncle Simon Whitcomb at Owasco just south of Auburn.

For unexplained reasons the Walkers were diverted here from their original objective, Alvah spent a week looking over the country along Cayuga Lake, visited the new state prison at Auburn, and attended a fair at Onondaga Hollow, while Vesta visited at Uncle Whitcomb's. They then turned their wagon around and drove to Syracuse, where they settled.

Syracuse was a brand-new village beginning to take shape on the uncompleted Erie Canal. It seemed to offer unlimited opportunities for a young carpenter. There is a tradition that Alvah erected the first frame house in Syracuse, and his employment soon ran the entire gamut of his trade. On Sundays the Walkers went to Baptist or Methodist services, and sometimes exchanged visits with the Furnisses and Whitcombs. Occasionally, Alvah found time to sketch or paint, and to read the Scriptures, the dictionary, or whatever fell into his hands, for he was an avid reader.

During the first winter Alvah was confined to his bed for days at a time suffering from complications following an attack of measles. Their first child, a son, was born the following June. He lived only a few days. Alvah made a small coffin and buried him. Vesta was gravely ill for several weeks, and Alvah finally carried her to her sister in Otisco, where she slowly recuperated.

The following winter Alvah was again sickly for weeks on end. He turned to carving clock cases and small chests for a livelihood. Faced with recurring illness, he began to read medical books, hoping to find a remedy for his delicate health. A by-product of this quest was his forswearing the joys of liquor and tobacco.

He also seems to have clarified his religious philosophy at this time. In the words of his son, Alvah, Jr., delivered more than a half century later at his father's funeral: "Though he devotedly hugged his faith in the atoning merits of Jesus, and answered to the creed and requirements of the Methodist Church sufficiently to retain a home with them, he never believed in a literal, future, burning Hell. . . . Many of you have often heard him say that everyone would enjoy hereafter the place or condition for which their earth life fitted them; [and] we saw in him a disposition to accept and advocate, regardless of all creeds, regardless of all issues, whatever [in his judgment] was right and true."

A second child, Vesta, arrived a year after the loss of their first-born, and then in order came Aurora, Luna, and Cynthia.

After ten years in Syracuse Alvah traded his home there for a thirty-three-acre farm, partially cleared, on the Bunker Hill Road

11

in Oswego Town, about five miles west of Oswego, New York. Here he felled the trees and built a house and barn. "He was one of the progressive and forehanded farmers of his day in Oswego Town, and at his own cost built and equipped the first schoolhouse to be erected in that town, giving the site for the same, his neighbors assisting in the erection of the building."[3] Later, when a district school was opened nearby, he converted it into the Universal Mechanic Shop, where he fashioned doors, sash, blinds, and coffins.

In 1868, when seventy, he patented a "water elevator" which, according to an advertisement, brought water from the bottom of the well, dumped a bucket of water into one's pail without waiting, permitted a child of six or seven years to draw a bucketful, whether the well was thirty or 200 feet deep, and could be rigged to bring water into the house.[4]

The advertisement also claimed that the water elevator had been awarded the highest premium at the New York State Fair and at several county fairs. But despite its glowing promises, it appears to have netted the inventor only meager returns. Despite his labor, Alvah was never quite able to pay off the mortgage on the property.

In moving to Oswego the Walkers settled on the periphery of a thriving community and, for the moment, one of the nation's boom towns. Six years before, a dam and hydraulic canal had harnessed the power of the Oswego River; four years earlier the Oswego Canal had linked the Erie Canal with Lake Ontario at the harbor of Oswego; and two years before the Welland Canal had joined Lake Ontario, Lake Erie, and the other Great Lakes. Briefly, Oswego rivaled Rochester, Buffalo and Syracuse in growth, and speculators scrambled to acquire land on the canals and harbor. One year prior to the arrival of the Walkers, Gerrit Smith had purchased an extensive tract on the east side of the harbor. He would soon be the city's largest property owner and business executive, and would also assume a considerable share of its conscience. In 1832 the population of the village was 3,000; by 1848 the newly created city totaled 11,000; and at the outset of the Civil War it stood at more than 17,000.

Three months after the Walkers settled on their farm another daughter was born, on November 26, 1832. They named her Mary Edwards for Alvah's maiden sister in Massachusetts. Mary thus started life in the Presidency of Andrew Jackson, the year of his dramatic battle with the Bank of the United States. Perhaps the colorful Old Hickory helped to endear the Democratic Party to her in later life.

A family of seven, then eight a year later, with the arrival of the first son on a farm newly cut from the wilderness, required innumerable chores, with the girls doing much of the work ordinarily done by boys. As a child, the slender, smallish, brown-haired Mary possessed the restless nervous energy which would sustain her through her long and often hectic life, and she was soon flitting around the premises under the tutelage of her mother and sisters. An early picture shows her wide-eyed and eager, with long curls falling below her shoulders.

Mary's home reflected the convictions of her much-traveled father. One of the less orthodox of these was that girls should be educated, and encouraged to pursue professional careers. Vesta, at eighteen, was licensed to teach in the common schools of the county. He believed, also, that their health should not be impaired by tight-fitting clothing. Years later Mary attested to her father's influence upon dress during her formative years, recalling that none of the daughters ever wore corsets at home. She also remembered his interest in medicine, and that she first dreamed of being a physician as she thumbed through his medical tracts. The Walkers were also Abolitionists, possibly the result of Alvah's inspection of slavery in Mississippi and Louisiana.

Incidentally, that the Walkers were not of the common mold may be illustrated also in the life of their son, Alvah H., or Alvie, as he was called, born a year after Mary. He supplemented farming with cabinet making and sleight of hand. During the winter months he traveled across central New York with a puppet show and as a ventriloquist. An agnostic, he delivered the funeral sermons for his parents in the little schoolhouse at Bunker Hill. An acquaintance once declared that it was a known fact that he had cursed an apple tree, and that it never again bore fruit.[5]

Mary received a common school education in the little one-room structure next door, and imbibed the intellectual stimulation of her home. Aurora and Luna attended Falley Seminary, an academy in Fulton, for two terms. Whether they commuted the ten miles or lived at the school is uncertain, but their study of natural philosophy, orthography, arithmetic, and grammar in-

13

evitably touched the household, and the training of the twelve-year-old Mary.

As an adolescent, Mary also was stirred by the intellectual climate of her youth. "Isms" blossomed in upstate New York in such profusion that itinerant preachers, who thrived on the frenzy of revivalism, but later bemoaned the utter exhaustion of the populace, labeled it the "burned-over-district." Meanwhile, Spiritualism, Abolitionism and Temperance had each won its converts. The first Woman's Rights Convention assembled at Seneca Falls in 1848, and the same year John Humphrey Noyes initiated a communistic, free-love colony at nearby Oneida. Not overlooked by the facile teen-ager was the Bloomerite movement, in which Amelia Jenks Bloomer and Elizabeth Smith Miller, daughter of Gerrit Smith, were leading advocates. Mary, though a country girl, could not have been oblivious to the publicity attending Mrs. Miller's first visit to Oswego in her bloomer regalia.

There were also the examples of George Sand, the French authoress and frequent wearer of masculine costumes, and the exotic adventuress, Lola Montez, who had dominated the government of Bavaria as the mistress of its prince, and who later toured America as an actress and advocate of women's rights. Mary owned an early edition of her best-selling *Lectures*.[6]

Mary toyed with the notion of a medical education for the missionary field, but a rocky farm and a large family precluded financial help from home. Instead, at eighteen, like her sisters, she attended Falley Seminary for two winter terms beginning in December, 1850. During the first term she was instructed in algebra, natural philosophy, and grammar and, surprisingly for a young woman, physiology and hygiene. The term lasted for fourteen weeks and ended in March. During the second term, shortened to seven weeks, she received what could have been only a smattering of algebra, arithmetic, Latin, and grammar. Now nineteen, she left the seminary in January, 1852, to take a teaching position in the village at Minetto, five miles from her home. She taught here for several years, saving as much as she could from her modest income. By this time her plans had crystallized; she would be a physician.

The medical profession to which she aspired in 1853 was a mélange of folkways upon which a variety of systems—products of the Romantic era—had been superimposed. Even a cursory glance at the medical practices of the time suggests this social lag, despite notable achievements in the natural sciences in this period. Still awaiting the germ theory of disease and the invention or application of scientific methods, a physician typically observed his patients without making use of a clinical thermometer or a stethoscope, or without taking the pulse.

Having made his diagnosis, he prescribed treatment in accordance with his preconceived acceptance of the nature of disease and its eradication. Still popular after more than a half-century, though losing ground to new schools of thought, was Benjamin Rush's (a signer of the Declaration of Independence) thesis that all diseases were, in reality, just one, resulting from "convulsive action." Treatment to "reduce" the action consisted of blood-letting (Washington had received this treatment on his death-bed) and purging, calomel serving as the favorite purge. If the convulsive action principle did not satisfy the physician, he might give at least lip service to one or more of the cults which had found popular favor. If he leaned toward the Thomsonians, and accepted their theory that the one great secret in health lay in the use of vegetable drugs, he would avoid calomel or salts and prescribe the "botanic system." Or, if he preferred vegetarianism with another twist, he might accept Sylvester Graham's formula: the avoidance of intemperance in foods and the use of whole-grain cereals to cure his patients. On the other hand, if he was convinced that bathing, inside and out, was the proper treatment for diseases, he might subscribe to hydropathy. And if none of these approaches satisfied him, he might try Mesmerism, Phrenology or Spiritualism, each of which had its adherents. The picture was not all black, however. Despite opposition from the public at large to vivisection, progress was being made in anatomy and physiology.

But medical education actually retrogressed during the early nineteenth century. The nation's rapid expansion westward and the phenomenal growth in population were not paralleled by a comparable growth in doctors. The older training centers such as Boston and Philadelphia proved inadequate, and the states chartered a host of medical colleges which offered shortened courses and cheapened degrees. By 1850, some were awarding diplomas for attendance at lectures through one winter.

Schools were generally classified according to their approach to healing: the Allopathic sought remedies which produced effects in contrast to the malady; the Homeopathic used drugs designed to produce in a healthy person symptoms similar to those manifested by the patient; the Eclectic accepted what seemed helpful from both the Allopathic and Homeopathic methods.

For Mary the situation was a blessing in disguise. The plethora of schools, and the resulting competition for students, induced a few institutions to open their doors to women. Several years earlier the Geneva Medical School had admitted Elizabeth Blackwell, and broken the sex barrier.

Mary gained admission to the Syracuse Medical College in December, 1853, just after her twenty-first birthday. The school had opened two years earlier with a faculty of nine practicing physicians, with a course of instruction consisting of three terms of thirteen weeks each. Between terms, students gained experience working with a practicing physician. It was thus not the shortest training offered, nor by any means the longest. It was identified as an Eclectic institution, and proclaimed the principle that "nothing should be used as a remedy that will injure the human constitution, and that all means used should have a direct tendency to sustain and not depress the vital powers." Incidentally, Mary's objections to amputations during the Civil War appear to have stemmed from this Eclectic doctrine.

At the Syracuse Medical College Mary received instruction in anatomy, surgery, the practice of medicine and medical pathology, obstetrics, and diseases of women and children; also physiology, materia medica, therapeutics and pharmacy, chemistry, and medical jurisprudence, a formidable but necessarily shallow potpourri of studies. Tuition was $55 a term, and there were fees of $5 for matriculation and $15 for graduation. Board and room cost about $1.50 a week.

Mary attended the winter and spring terms of 1853-1854, and the winter term of 1854-1855, completing the course despite problems relating to her sex and finances, and received a medical degree in June, 1855, the only woman in her class. Thus at twenty-two she was one of a handful of female practitioners.

She launched her medical career in Columbus, Ohio, where her father's sister, Harriet Walker Hall, had settled. However, a few months' trial demonstrated that Ohioans were reluctant to entrust their aches and pains to a woman. A letter to Mary while in Columbus from a seamstress and former schoolmate suggests the adjustment Mary was facing as a novice in a new community. "How do you enjoy yourself so far from home?" she asked. "Do you have much practice; and do you like the profession? I think you would tire of it, when it comes to being called up at any time of the night."[7] Unfortunately, Mary's reply has been lost.

Returning to New York State, Mary offered her services to the people of Rome with greater but not unqualified success.

In retrospect, it would appear that Mary's bid for acceptance by the public was doomed from the start. The prejudice facing any female physician was a formidable handicap. But she intensified these doubts and reservations by assuming personality traits and a behavioral pattern which tended to set her apart from her townspeople.

For one thing, upon her arrival at Rome she no longer dressed like most other women. During her medical training she had experimented with her dress, seeking to simplify it to provide a more practical costume for her profession. She soon adopted the bloomer fad, with a tunic or coat-dress reaching below the knees. The few original recruits to bloomers, it might be added, were already reverting to traditional ground-touching skirts. This unorthodoxy identified her as a militant feminist, and undoubtedly closed many doors to her.

Her marital experience at this time served to further emphasize her peculiarities. At medical school she met Albert Miller, a fellow student from Cortland County. It appears to have been love at first sight, or almost. Albert was quite a catch for a girl with a rural background and limited social advantages. A few years older than his classmates, he was recognized as a gifted scholar and orator. He was chosen by the faculty to address the alumni at the graduation exercises. Speaking upon "The True Thinker," he proclaimed that all true eclectics were free thinkers.[8] Gregarious and out-going, he cut a dashing figure at the school, and his special attentions to Mary must have been a thrilling experience for her.

At graduation they parted, Albert establishing a practice at Rome, N.Y., while Mary went off to Ohio to what proved to be a trial period of but a few months. It was undoubtedly Albert's proposal of marriage and a common medical practice which terminated her stay in Columbus.

17

A few days after her return to Oswego, Mary and Albert were married at the Walker home on Bunker Hill. Indicative that the union was not altogether conventional was the choice of the minister. Mary passed over the local Methodist clergyman to select the Rev. Mr. Samuel J. May, a noted liberal Unitarian theologian and Abolitionist of Syracuse, to perform the ceremony. The bride contributed a further touch of unorthodoxy when she appeared in trousers and a dress-coat; and convention was flaunted again, when the bride's obligation to obey her spouse was stripped from the ritual. As Mary explained later, "Men who meritoriously wear the name of men are becoming too common-sensified to advocate any such slavishness. The noble Rev. Mr. May would not stoop to such despicable meanness as to ask a woman to 'serve' or 'obey' a man. How barbarous the very idea of one equal promising to be the slave of another, instead of both entering life's greatest drama as intelligent equal parties. Our promises were such as denoted two intelligent beings instead of one intelligence and one chained."[9] A final challenge to tradition was apparent in the bride's insistence upon retaining her maiden name. Her only concession was an occasional inclusion of Miller or "M" before Walker. Thus she sometimes signed her name Miller-Walker, or Dr. Mary E. M. Walker, but never Dr. Mary E. Miller, or Mrs. Albert Miller.

Perhaps Mary's personality ruled out the usual conjugal relationship. But for several years she lived with Albert, first at 76 Dominick Street, and later at 60 Dominick Street, where they also had their offices. At the outset Mary appears to have been an affectionate wife, anxious to please and assist her husband. She took charge of the house and directed the housekeeper and, in addition, attended to her profession. A friend later testified that "her whole appearance was that of a noble, self-reliant, business woman, and also an affectionate wife." But wedded bliss ended suddenly, when she received reports that Albert was unfaithful. She confronted him, and he admitted the charge. She declared that she would not live with him, and would seek a divorce. Whereupon her philandering mate retorted that if she would refrain, she "might have the same privileges."[10]

It was not the kind of equality Mary was advocating. She ordered Albert from the house, and he departed in haste. As he drove away he encountered the acquaintance, mentioned above, and shouted angrily to him that he was going away, and not returning. When the startled friend went inside and asked Mary what Dr. Miller meant by his ill-tempered remark, she burst into tears.

Whether this parting was the final separation or just a prelude to it remains unanswered. Some years later, Albert said that in September, 1859, he sold a part of the furniture, dismissed the housekeeper, closed his part of the office, and left Rome. In any event, Mary was living alone in March, 1860, when she moved from 60 Dominick Street to smaller quarters a few doors down the street.

The months immediately following this removal to 48 Dominick Street are of interest in appraising her professional services at this time, for they supply the only records available. Though scant, they provide a few insights. In a period of just over five months, between March and August, 1860, Mary appears to have netted a gross income of about $108, and incurred expenditures of $140, leaving a deficit of $32. Among her expenditures were sums of $63 for board and rent, $40 for clothing, travel and miscellaneous personal items, and $35 for office expenses. Included among the latter were totals of $7.69 for medicine, $2 for a sign at her doorway, and $9.63 for a portrait and frame for a diploma and a picture, office decoration for the period thus costing more than medical supplies! There is no record of accounts payable to her, however, so that it cannot be stated conclusively that she was losing money. However, the volume is low, and it would appear that she was edging toward a precarious existence. On the other hand, expenditures for trips, one to Waterloo to attend a convention with a round-trip cost of $5.50, and for portraits and frames would not suggest dire poverty.

In one instance she rendered medical service in return for the rental of a horse and buggy. A single entry in the ledger spells out the specific medical service: an extraction of a tooth for a fee of 25¢.[11]

A small advertisement in the Rome *Sentinel* reporting the change of address mentioned above offers no doubts about future operations:

FEMALE PHYSICIAN

Dr. Mary Walker has removed to No. 48 Dominick Street opposite the "Arcade," over Messrs. H. S. & W. O. Shelleys' Clothing Store.

19

The Doctor expresses her gratitude to the Romans for their liberal patronage, and solicits a continuance of the same.

Office first door at the right up stairs.

Office hours from 7 to 8 A.M., and from 1 to 3 and 6 to 8 P.M.

Mary E. M. Walker, M.D.

Rome, March 8th, 1860.[12]

At the head of the "classified" column, the *Sentinel* added its comments to the advertisement:

> Reference is made to the advertisement of Dr. Mary Walker, Female Physician, who, it will be seen, has removed her office to the rooms over Messrs. Shelleys' Clothing Store. As there is generally alleged to be so much rivalry and jealousy between those of the medical profession, we hardly dare to venture to give one of them a "puff," even by way of preference over the other. Those, however, who prefer the skill of a female physician to that of the male, have now an excellent opportunity to make their choice.

The above editorial comment hints at a situation which went far beyond Mary's bid to succeed in the medical profession. The number and variety of physicians competing for the public's favor posed a financial problem for many of them. It was not uncommon at this time for medics to abandon their profession in search of more lucrative employment.

Some years later, when asked about her experience at Rome, Mary's response indicated a pride of achievement. Some people sent for her, she said, because they had confidence in her skill; others, because they thought it was a woman's business to prescribe for women. She had planned to limit her practice to women and children, but if a woman begged her to see her husband, she had not felt at liberty to refuse. She insisted that she had saved the lives of some who had first laughed at her, and had performed many operations. While she seems to have exaggerated her experience in surgery, there is no question but that she concentrated more seriously upon medicine during these years in Rome than at any other period of her life.

CHAPTER II

A CRUSADER FOR DRESS REFORM

Marriage and medical practice by no means absorbed the young physician's interests. She had scarcely settled down in Rome when she was caught up in a broader movement to spread dress reform among the millions of benighted women. Opportunity came in the guise of the *Sibyl,* a new fortnightly woman's magazine, and its dynamic editor, Dr. Lydia Sayer Hasbrouck, journalist, physician, and dress reformer of Middletown, New York.

In fact, her contact with this truly remarkable personality was one of the turning points of her life. A native of Orange County, New York, and just five years older than Mary, Lydia Sayer had joined the Bloomerites in 1849 but, unlike most of her early associates in the movement, wore them throughout her life. Rejected for admittance by an academy because of her unorthodox dress, she turned to medicine for a career and began to practice in Washington just a year before Mary received her diploma at Syracuse. She was soon lecturing and writing, and in 1856 removed to Middletown to join John S. Hasbrouck in publishing the *Sibyl.* The first issue, on June 1, indicated that it would be a "Review of Tastes, Errors and Fashions of Society." In the fourth issue the editors announced their marriage by common-law ceremony in which each had repeated an acceptance of the other. Dr. Hasbrouck was a national leader of dress reform, temperance, and woman's suffrage for the next half-century.

Mary seems to have been one of the *Sibyl's* original subscribers, and was soon serving as agent for its sale in Rome and at gatherings of dress reformers. In its thirteenth issue on January 1, 1857, she broke into print when she contributed the first of what was to become a series of communications. In a letter to the editor, she hailed the imminence of a dress reform convention at Canastota in January, 1857, where she anticipated a "good attendance of those who were richly provided with common sense, intelligence and decision of character."

The following issue of the magazine featured the second of Mary's letters: a resumé of the convention. Though not the secretary or responsible for publicity, her letter was the first and only report received by the *Sibyl* before press time, and Dr. Hasbrouck added her personal thanks for it. Her letter revealed that the convention had agreed not to accept a fixed pattern of clothing; also, that all of the speakers with one exception were dressed in short skirts. It also revealed that Mary had made a small contribution to the program, a demonstration of the advantages of the short dress with a live model clad in the bloomer-tunic ensemble.

In the months which followed Mary wrote of a female physician in Cleveland, Ohio, who saved the life of a man given up as lost by male practitioners. "She [the woman] will continue to attend to the duties of the profession, and soon wear laurels which he [man] may not handle, and hold a palm that he can never wrest from her. The brighter the moon shines, the louder some dogs bark."[1] She also offered liberal quotations in another article from what she lauded as an enlightened sermon on the rights and duties of Christian women by a Methodist minister in Rome. She praised the minister as a liberal man, and predicted that the truths contained could not fail to clean away some of the "old fogeyism."[2]

Mary's contributions to the *Sibyl* earned a place for her on the program of the second convention of what was now termed the Reform-Dress Association, at Syracuse. The magazine's reporter judged it brief, but excellent.[3] Incidentally, the dress reform was catching on. Almost 100 of the participants and spectators wore the abbreviated skirt in a variety of styles.

In December, 1857, the *Sibyl* revealed that Mary had launched a career as a lecturer, having spoken on dress reform at Black River, a village near Watertown, New York. "The lecturer acquitted herself in a very easy, graceful manner," it reported, "and exhibited familiarity with the science connected with her profession. She insisted that woman should make herself better acquainted with her own physical organization that she might be better enabled to preserve her own health. . . . She spoke disparagingly of the tight and cumbrous clothing usually worn by women. She manifested a great desire to be useful to her sex, and undoubtedly has it in her power to do much good." More significant for the future than the favorable publicity was the experience itself, for, excepting her participation in the dress-reform convention, it may have been her first venture upon the platform. It was a long step from the one-room school, and a significant departure from her medical practice.

A short time later a letter published in an Oswego paper furnished a vehicle for another of Mary's columns in the *Sibyl*. Titled "A Bloomer in the Street" and signed "X," the Oswego letter reported that "a young lady of modest and graceful bearing and of more than ordinary *beauty*," had been seen on the Oswego streets dressed in bloomers. It had brought out a crowd, which she might have found pleasing. Yet, "how sadly she was deceived in cheating a graceful form and carriage of the flowing drapery of her sex." After quoting the letter, Mary turned her invective, a weapon she was to sharpen with more deadly effect with the passage of time, upon the hapless "X." She denied that the wearer of the bloomers, whom she identified as Adalene Parsons Whittlesy of Lewis County, was "deceived," or that she was a "martyr." The real martyrs, she insisted, were the poor devotees of fashion. Dress reformers could testify to the fact, for they had tried both modes and found the bloomer superior.

Mr. "X's" admiration for the "graceful carriage" was easy to explain, for how was it possible for a lady loaded down with crinoline to walk with the "ease and grace" displayed by Mrs. Whittlesy, she asked. The contrast between the latter and the "hugely crinolined Oswegonians" was obvious. "She has cheated her graceful form and carriage of the flowing drapery of her sex; yes, and she has cheated the grave of its victim, when it supposed that it would soon open its portals to receive its victim." Mr. "X" had erred also in referring to the wearer of bloomers as a young lady, she continued. In reality, she was thirty years of age, and had worn the bloomers for several years. "No wonder you made such a mistake when you saw how easily she walked, relieved of a surplus amount of clothing. Cease your lamentations over the bloomers, brother 'X'!"[4]

Subsequently, she directed her attention to the Sickles-Key murder and scandal in Washington, upset by what she considered biased reporting, which implied that a female's vice was more reprehensible than a male's. "Never until women are better educated physiologically, until they are considered something besides a drudge or a doll—until they have all of the social, educational and political advantages that men enjoy—in a word, equality with men, shall we consider vice in our sex more culpable than in man." She urged women to "throw aside their embroidery, and read Mental Philosophy, Moral Science and Physiology, and then go to a smith's and have their dressical and dietitical chains severed that they may go forth free, sensible women."[5]

She then wrote a sequel, prophesying that women in the future would be educated similarly to men; and when the Mount Vernon Ladies' Association proposed an endowment of $500,000 to restore the home of George Washington, she made a counterproposal that the sum be used to finance a "grand national literary female college." "How much more noble to educate the immortal mind to build monuments that are self-moving and progressive, than to build monuments that are continually casting superstitions over the nation," she advised in one of her more eloquent passages. Mount Vernon, she insisted, could never be more than a "house and tomb."[6]

She devoted additional letters to plead for the establishment of a New York State Foundling Hospital. An asylum for "morally unfortunate women," she argued, was as much needed as homes for the deaf and dumb, the blind, the insane and the inebriate. She decried the futility of the old laws against abortion and infanticide, and was indignant over the difference in treatment accorded the errant woman, and the man who was equally guilty.[7]

Incidentally, Mary's mother, an avid reader of the *Sibyl*, was stimulated, doubtless by her daughter's example, to direct a letter to this journal to report a recent occurrence in Greenwich, Massachusetts, her childhood home. Titled "Let Your Women Keep Silent," it noted that a woman filled with religion arose in a Presbyterian prayer meeting and spoke her mind. It was considered so sinful that the minister dismissed the meeting when she sat down. Later a male member of the congregation, speculating upon the sinfulness of the times, proposed that women be permitted to speak, and thereby exert a moral influence. The divine agreed that it might make prayer circles more interesting, but that it was obviously prohibited by the Scriptures.[8]

She did not editorialize; none was needed.

The results of Mary's venture into journalism can hardly be exaggerated. She wrote her first letter with some trepidation to remind readers of a local convention. Three years later she was discussing issues basic to woman's rights. At the fourth annual meeting of what was now heralded as the National Dress Reform Association, meeting at Waterloo, New York, in the spring of 1860, she was elected the third of nine vice-presidents. At the evening session in the absence of the president she was asked to preside, but she declined, preferring to participate actively in the discussion.

In late summer of 1860 the twenty-seven-year-old physician and dress reformer decided to make her recent separation from her husband permanent through an Iowa divorce. She seems to have made up her mind precipitously. There is no hint of it in her business journal, with its record of new quarters and furnishings; nor is there any clue among her columns in the *Sibyl*. The New York law may have appeared too formidable, where only adultery was a legal ground for divorce, or possibly she shunned the unfavorable publicity which a divorce would have produced. Perhaps it was both her resentment toward Dr. Miller and her slender medical practice which impelled her. In any event, she was off to Delhi, then the county seat of Delaware County in eastern Iowa.

There is no mystery attached to her selection of this distant village. It was the residence of A. F. House, a young lawyer recently removed from Oswego, and a friend of the Walker family. She lived for a time with the House family, and thirty years ago older residents recalled that they had seen the diminutive Bloomerite during her sojourn there.

At Delhi she made her presence known to the publisher of the local newspaper, who had defended her bloomer costume in his columns after it had been ridiculed by the press in Dubuque. Fairness, he had asserted, demanded that they cease "sneering at her for wearing a dress unfashionably too short at the bottom, unless they likewise lashed some of their own ladies for wearing dresses fashionably too short at the top." Furthermore, he argued, Miss Walker was one of the few women upon whom a bloomer dress could be made to "hang right." "We have seen bloomers on short, fat, dumpy women, which made them look at a distance like a beer keg balanced on a couple of corks . . . but Miss Walker is just the size and style to look well in a bloomer dress."

The editor's kind words, of course, endeared him to Mary, who poured out the story of her life for him. Later, he recalled that while she appeared to be about 25 to 28 years old, the many achievements which she cited as a teacher, medical student, physician, dress reformer, and editor would have required close to 120 years. He also remembered that she had agreed to write a column for his paper, but that he soon discovered that she offered little except her "own doings" to gratify her vanity or spite; also, that she "triumphantly and unconsciously over-rode all rules of grammar, punctuation and capitalization."[9]

The months of inactivity in Delhi must have weighed heavily upon Mary's restive spirits. Unable to endure the boredom, she resolved to resume her study of German. An entry in her journal in Rome on May 21, 1860, "A German A.B.C. Book, 13 cents," suggests that she had initiated the project there. Hence she entered the fall term of the Bowen Collegiate Institute at Hopkinton, thirteen miles from Delhi. The institute had opened its doors a year before, and was struggling to perpetuate itself despite serious financial problems.

Mary had barely settled down with her ninety-five fellow students when she was the center of controversy. It turned out that the overworked faculty was not prepared to offer German, despite its inclusion in the school's prospectus. Mary threatened to go to court to require a fulfillment of their obligation. And while the pot was boiling, she attempted to enroll in a class in rhetoric which was provided for the gentlemen. The directress, a Miss Cooley, who opposed the idea of young ladies declaiming, refused the request unconditionally.

An old history of Delhi County offers a concise and colorful account of the impass:

> Mary began to work upon the young men to obtain their help to secure the coveted privilege of going on the rostrum, and readily secured their sympathy. She was then ready for mischief, and announced to the teachers that she had come to study German, and that if they did not provide her a teacher she would publish far and wide that they were advertising what they did not and could not perform. Meanwhile, the young men of the village had organized a debating society, and Mary attended one evening. She was a faithful listener

and, before the meeting closed, called for the reading of the by-laws, and asked to be admitted a member. She was promptly voted in, and assigned a place in the debate for the next meeting. This came to the ears of the faculty, and Miss Cooley ordered her not to attend. Mary went, however, taking her place in the discussion, but with indifferent success. The next day, at Miss Cooley's request, Miss Mary was suspended, and all the young men but two valorously gathered up their books and left with her. They formed a procession in front of the building, marched down town with the little mischief-maker at their head, and paraded several streets. The young men were also suspended, but soon repented, and asked for permission to go back, stipulating, however, that their Amazonian captain should be allowed to return also; but this was refused. The young men then surrendered unconditionally, and Mary was permanently suspended. The young woman remained for some time afterward, and assisted Dr. Cunningham occasionally in his practice. A few other citizens befriended her for a time. Her portrait is preserved, and indicates a rather pretty face. Her dress was then, as now, of the most pronounced Bloomer type.[10]

Unfortunately, no one seems to have taken a photograph of the tiny Amazon as she led the students down the main street of Hopkinton.

Mary was back in Rome in May or June of 1861. For reasons unexplained, she had not secured a divorce. In a column in the *Sibyl,* after a conspicuous absence for almost a year, she explained that pressing business would not permit her to attend the annual convention of the dress reformers. She wished them success, and praised the *Sibyl* for its effective leadership.

She did not define the nature of her business, but from other sources it is evident that she had initiated action for a divorce in New York State. She secured a favorable decision in the Supreme Court of Madison County in September, but the decree was not finalized. Again, her failure may have been her unwillingness to wait it out, and after the Civil War interlude, she had to begin a third time.

27

She obtained a special act of the legislature in 1866, permitting her to subtract her war years from the elapsed time since her separation so as to evade the statute of limitations (five years), and finally in 1869 she was declared legally free from her long-estranged husband. Her witnesses, it might be added, pictured Albert as a Lothario with an almost endless sequence of seductions. He seems to have had an enviable bedside manner!

There was no subsequent reconciliation, though as late as 1865 Albert wrote a friendly letter to Lyman Coats, husband of Mary's sister, Aurora, inquiring after Mary's welfare. He declared that he regretted the separation, and would help Mary if she were in need. What was done in haste was not necessarily right, and it sometimes required years of trial and sorrow to find the truth.[11]

Mary was not favorably impressed by Albert's belated offer of the olive branch. "I wish you would tell Lyman," she instructed her mother from Albany, "that if that *villain* writes again [to him] or *any one*, under any pretense whatever, to forward any such letter to me, and not to answer *under any consideration*.

"Should he, the vile Miller, ever come around anywhere, don't let him in the house."[12]

And later, when she carefully arranged her divorce papers, and filed them away, she inscribed on the packet, "Divorce and last letter of the villain."[13]

She seldom spoke of her unhappy married experience, and in time many of her acquaintances doubted that she had ever been wedded. Once, when she appeared as a witness in court, a judge —presumably for the court's amusement—attempted to ferret out the details of her nuptials. Only after a lengthy huddle with her attorney did she concede that she had been married. She would not elaborate.

The broken marriage undoubtedly contributed to her cynicism, and to her low esteem for the human male. It also etched her eccentricities a bit more sharply.

CHAPTER III

ONE WOMAN'S WORK IN THE CIVIL WAR

When the Civil War suddenly created a demand for physicians and surgeons, Mary's practice in Rome was scarcely a deterrent, and she was off to Washington, bloomers and all, shortly after the Battle of Bull Run. The niche which she chose for herself was nothing less than a commission as surgeon in the army; but, without waiting for the outcome of her petition, she volunteered to help wherever she was needed. Finding that there was a dearth of doctors, she simply made herself useful, and was soon ministering to the sick and wounded. Meanwhile, her application for a commission was rejected; the Surgeon General was not prepared to break tradition by appointing a female. And thus Mary's informal status continued from month to month, and year to year.

The war was one of the happiest epochs in her kaleidoscopic career. Rebuffs from top brass did not obviate the fact that she was needed almost anywhere she chose to open her medical case. An appraisal of her services is difficult, since many of the details must be drawn from her reminiscences, which appear to have expanded with the telling.

However, it is evident that she went to Washington in October, and volunteered her services at a makeshift hospital set up in the United States Patent Office. Dr. J. N. Green, the surgeon in charge, was impressed by her hustle, and was soon using her as an administrative assistant.

Later, Mary called on the Surgeon General, Clement A. Finley, seeking a more formal appointment as assistant acting surgeon. But Finley, who made no attempt to veil his dislike for contract surgeons, and who would soon be dismissed for his failure to work with the United States Sanitary Commission, gave her a quick refusal. She next went to Assistant Surgeon General R. C. Wood who, according to her account of the interview, was favorably impressed with her qualifications, and Dr. Green's recommendation, but would not act against the wishes of his superior in office.

29

Undaunted, Mary returned to her duties at the Patent Office Hospital, where she cared for Indiana troops housed there as an assistant physician and surgeon without title. She found the work exhilarating, despite the absence of her name from the payroll.

"Every soul in the hospital has to abide by my orders, as much as though Dr. Green gave them," she noted with obvious pride. "And not a soldier can go out of the building after stated hours, without a pass from him or myself."[1]

She was intrigued with the gleaming marble of the unfinished Patent Office, "warmed with hot air and well lighted with gas that burns all night," and the thousands of patents ranging from medicines to engines, and the personal effects of George Washington on display there.

When not on duty her avid curiosity led her around the capital city and across the Potomac to the line of forts taking shape along the Virginia front between Arlington and Alexandria. It was challenging and satisfying after the frustrations of her marriage and medical practice.

During the months which followed she offered her services without stint. She was a hospital administrator, therapist, counselor, amanuensis, expediter and confessor: a wounded soldier, unable to write, and wishing to dictate a letter to his family; separated from his comrades, and seeking to be returned; homesick, and desirous of a mother's attentions; war fatigued, and needing recreation; facing an amputation and lacking courage; nearing death, and seeking consolation. These and similar situations crowded her days and competed for her attention.

She found that her volunteer status was sometimes advantageous, in that it permitted her to drop lesser duties to handle more pressing matters. For example, she took time to escort a desperately wounded soldier personally to his home in Rhode Island, where he could secure the tender affections of his loved ones. Later, she made a similar mission to Ravenna, Ohio, where she paused long enough to deliver a lecture, a benefit performance, for the Soldiers' Aid Society.

In her "Notes on the War," Mary described a visit by Dorothea Dix to the hospital while she was acting assistant surgeon. When the famous reformer, now Superintendent of Female Nurses of the United States, spotted Mary, she appeared troubled. Mary could think of no explanation at the time, but when she learned

30

later that the prim Dorothea would accept only women who were past thirty, who were healthy, "plain almost to repulsion in dress and devoid of personal attractions," she attributed her scowl to her disapproval at finding "a young and goodlooking woman" in the hospital. "But as she could not possibly have any control over me, she walked through the hospital in a manner hard to describe. When she saw a patient who was too ill to arrange the clothing on his cot, if it became disarranged and a foot was exposed, she turned her head the other way, seeming not to see the condition, while I was so disgusted with such sham modesty that I hastened to arrange the soldier's bed clothing, if I chanced to be near when no nurses were to do this duty." Mary acknowledged Miss Dix's contributions to the care of the insane, but considered her attitude toward young woman nurses indefensible.[2]

A second anecdote from her war recollections would appear to border on the tall tale. While strolling from the Patent Office Hospital one hot evening in search of fresh air, a dude approached her, and asked where she was going. Mary was well prepared for the encounter, having a six-shooter tucked inside her jacket. In what would have required split-second timing she resolved to make an example of him. She drew the revolver from her pocket, aimed it at the startled assailant, and shouted that she was ready to kill six just like him. He beat a hasty retreat, glancing back from time to time to be certain that it was not a bad dream. Amused at his discomfort, Mary fired a shot into the ground.

She was almost immediately surrounded by questioners, including a policeman, seeking to determine the cause of the shot. "I fired the ball," she replied, "for the purpose of giving those dudes to understand upon what ground I stood, believing that those of this class who believe that there are no women capable of taking care of themselves when young, would inform their friends that they might be in danger of their lives if they approached me. I was never spoken to again in an impertinent manner in my walks thereafter."

Contributing to Mary's effectiveness in a war emergency, though frequently a source of irritation in peace time, was her assertiveness. If a situation required attention, or if a wrong could be righted, she pressed for action, let the chips fall where they might. To a well-meaning clergyman, who asked what he could do for the soldiers at the hospital, Mary replied that he might supply checkerboards. Then, as the significance of checkers for therapy blossomed in her mind, she requested that he supply them to all the hospitals in Washington. The clergyman eventually provided some hundreds of the games before Mary would call off the search.[3]

On another occasion, according to Mary's "Notes," when appeals from alleged deserters imprisoned in the Deserters' Prison in Alexandria reached her attention, she decided to go to the prison to hear their stories. When she sought admission, she was refused by the guard. Drawing herself up to her full five feet, she countered with no little emphasis, "I am Dr. Walker of the Union Army. I command you to let me pass." The surprised guard stepped aside, and Mary had her interviews. She was soon convinced that several of the men were unjustly confined; one boy, for example, had slipped away from his regiment to see his dying mother. She went directly to the War Office, and to Secretary Stanton, for their release, protocol weighing lightly upon her. She had the satisfaction of obtaining a pardon for the above-mentioned prisoner, and a pass and escort for him.[4]

While at the hospital at the Patent Office, she became convinced that surgeons were amputating unnecessarily, in some cases for practice rather than from necessity. Knowing that a protest to higher authority would bring down the wrath of the surgeons upon her, and possibly result in her dismissal, she connived with the soldiers involved to have them refuse to submit to surgery; and if this did not suffice, to threaten reprisals and even bodily harm, should the surgeon persist. She seems to have been oblivious of the professional ethics involved.[5]

Again, observing that hundreds of women who flocked to Washington to visit sons and husbands could find no accommodations, and were forced to spend their nights in parks or on the streets, she jumped into the breach, and was instrumental in organizing the Women's Relief Association, designed to raise funds to aid women in this predicament. As secretary of the group she promoted a series of benefits, and on at least several occasions delivered the principal address. She also appealed to women of wealth to aid the cause. The campaign was soon broadened to encompass destitute women, whatever the source of their embarrassment. Recognizing that no two cases were alike, she instituted a system of counseling, "that their necessities and the *causes* of the same might be considered."[6]

The drive was a marked success. The chairman of the Congressional committee for the District of Columbia, at their bidding, opened a house for "Unprotected females and children who are frequently found about the streets of Washington without friends, money or home," on Tenth Street near Ford's Theater. When this proved inadequate, Mary made her own home at 374 Ninth Street available, and stocked it with surplus materials which she solicited from the commissary of the army. In the course of several years, in addition to her work as secretary, she was president, medical officer and manager of the home. But with pressing army duties to fulfill early in 1864, she resigned as president, and published a short note in the *National Republican* in defence of her withdrawal from active association with the cause. She had donated her services; "Now there were others that have become interested, who are directly or indirctly being supported by the Government. . . . My heart is still with the cause, but my energies must be in another direction."[7]

Her work had anticipated that of the Women's Christian Association, the Women's Hospital, and the Soldiers' Orphan Home.

Some time early in 1862 Mary left the Patent Office Hospital to serve for a short time at the Forest Hall Prison in Georgetown. As at the Patent Office, the arrangement was completely informal, and when she was no longer needed, or possibly tired of it, she moved out.

Lacking duties in Washington, she went to New York to qualify for another medical diploma at the Hygeia Therapeutic College. The school was sufficiently unorthodox to include a woman on its staff, Dr. Huldah Page, who was a professor of physiology, hygiene, and obstetrics. Instruction included lectures and a few clinics at Bellevue Hospital. Mary's studies could have been little more than a refresher, but she departed with a medical degree dated March 31, 1862.[8]

During this lull in her activities in Washington Mary found time to resume her letters to the *Sibyl*. The first was a rambling reappraisal of her experiences with the reform dress after more than five years of use. Her silence, she reassured her readers, did not mean that she had returned to conventional garb. Not at all!

She had worn it in ten states and Canada, and had continued to find that its comfort, convenience, and healthfulness overbalanced the petty annoyances from those who were ignorant of its principles or lacked the moral courage to adopt it.

If wearers of the reform dress should seek a more formal name for the costume, she was prepared to recommend "the Littlejohn Dress." In Delhi, Iowa, she reported, she had met a Mrs. Littlejohn, who had worn black broadcloth pants on an overland trip to Oregon more than twenty years before, making her the earliest on record. She had made the journey as a missionary from New England, and had worn the reform dress since that time.[9]

Mary repeated her defence of the reform dress in a second letter, and a short time later devoted a column to "The Noble Men in the Army."

In October, 1862, she was home in Oswego, where she delivered a lecture at the Music Hall on the current scene in Washington. The original draft of this address, with scattered insertions and strike-outs for use on other occasions, is in the Walker papers. It was largely factual: a bird's eye view of the capital city. Beginning with the historical background, she proceeded to the streets, parks and bridges. She gave particular emphasis to the Capitol building, covering its construction and its unfinished wings and dome in minute detail. But she occasionally departed from stone and mortar to the functions of the House of Representatives, Senate and Supreme Court; also the Congressional Library, then housed in the Capitol.

She also gave special attention to the President's residence (which she did not refer to as the White House), described the uses of the various rooms, and offered her impressions of a Presidential reception. She pictured Lincoln as "cordial," but added that he seemed "not to unduly feel the dignity of his position." Mary Lincoln was "well-proportioned, fair, round-faced, lively, and pleasing."

She dwelt at length upon the wonders of the Patent Office and the Smithsonian Institution, and more briefly upon the Treasury Building, the National Armory, and the National Observatory. She mentioned the General Post Office and Benjamin Franklin, the first Postmaster, as a prop to emphasize that the office had employed women for more than a year at $500 per annum.

She closed with a survey of the hospitals, lauding the services of the female nurses. They were women of sterling character, graduates of seminaries and colleges, and dedicated to a glorious cause. "What if such are slandered by those who have not the moral courage to step outside of time-honored customs, when our nation is in peril?" Except for the brief allusion to women in the postoffice, it was her only reference to women's rights, and at its conclusion she added, "Pardon the digression." She never apologized for defending women again![10]

After the lecture Mary returned to Washington, the local press explaining that she planned to look after the soldiers of the Oswego County regiments, and that she would reply promptly to inquiries, if accompanied by return postage. The article implies that she had no other commitments.

A few weeks later, however, she was at the headquarters of General Burnside near Warrenton, Virginia, where she had gone to see if she could be of service. She found that there were several cases of typhoid fever, that medical supplies were inadequate, and that the medical staff was undermanned and exhausted. "I went to my trunk," she recalled in her "Notes," "took out four pretty nightgowns, tore them into small squares; and taking them into the hospital, told the soldier nurses how to apply them to the temples of the sufferers."[11]

She visited the battlefield at Manassas, and the village of Warrenton, where she saw secessionists at first hand. It is difficult to say who was more curious: Virginians, as they beheld Mary, now clad in a blue officer's uniform, pants with gold stripes, a felt hat encircled by a golden cord, and the green sash of a surgeon; or Mary, as her roving eyes caught the myriad details of Southern village life. She was impressed by the signs of poverty and scarcity, the armies having taken off much of their substance, and in particular by the conditions in the Warren Green Hotel, the "*first class* hotel in the Rebel Village," where she remained overnight. She found the furnishings sparse, the bedding worn and inadequate, the locks in the doors without keys, and the board costly, at two dollars a day.[12]

Convinced that the sick would receive better care in Washington, she went to headquarters and urged their removal. General Burnside agreed to her plan, and authorized her to accompany them. Before the order could be executed, however, the army moved out, amidst rumors that the "Rebels" were cutting the railroad and attacking the guard between the camp and Washington. A scramble ensued among the camp followers, including governmental officials and unattached officers, who had come down from the capital, for transportation back to the District. They had soon appropriated a locomotive and most of the rolling stock, but Mary managed to crowd the patients on the last six cars.

Ready to relax from a job well done, she waited for the locomotive to start them on their way. It did not budge. Growing impatient, she investigated, and found that all in authority had departed. "So I stepped up to the engineer, and asked why he didn't start. 'I have no authority,' said he. 'Then I will give you orders,' I replied. 'Start at once for Washington. Oh yes, I have the authority,' and I waved at him my letter from General Burnside." The engineer relented, and the train started. Mary advised him to run slowly and carefully to avoid jolting the injured. En route, she ministered to them, moving from car to car. At Alexandria the engineer stopped the cars, and declared that he could not proceed to Washington without orders. Mary repeated her commands, and added for good measure that, if he refused, she would see that his case was reported to the War Department. The train lurched forward, and stopped again only when it had reached its destination. Two of the stricken had died en route.[18]

She later added the following anecdote, illustrative of her status in the army. At their arrival in Washington, the ladies of the city were on hand to offer food and drink to the injured, but when she asked for a sandwich for herself she was refused. She was told that the food was for soldiers. Only after a spirited explanation did they permit the indignant Mary to share in the food.

After catching her breath in Washington, Mary was again in a tent hospital in December. She needed the respite, for near Falmouth, just across the Rappahannock River from Fredericksburg, she labored day and night to aid the thousands of wounded pouring in from the Battle of Fredericksburg, one of the ghastliest slaughters of the war.

In her many references to war experiences Mary seems to have never referred specifically to performing surgery. Nor does it appear that she served regularly as a physician. Undoubtedly the uniqueness of her situation, a lone woman medic in an army of men, as well as her status as a volunteer, militated against such an assignment. Furthermore, her pre-war experience as a surgeon

36

was extremely limited. It would seem, therefore, that except in emergencies, such as in this field hospital at Fredericksburg, her duties more nearly paralleled those of a nurse or a hospital administrator, than a practicing physician or surgeon. But on these occasions, at least, she saw the horrors of war, and did what she could to alleviate the suffering.

The field hospitals could ignore only the dying, and move those with minor wounds or sicknesses to the rear, while they stanched the flow of blood and eased the pain of those whose injuries fell between the two extremes. Opium pills were given to ease shock, and later in the war morphine, administered by a hypodermic syringe, served a similar purpose. The hurried operations violated every principle of modern asepsis, and the resulting infection was taken for granted. The hospitals reeked with chloroform, the favorite anesthetic; carbolic acid was sometimes used in dressing wounds, but was usually applied only after infection. Most wounds were inflicted on the arms and legs, and the usual treatment was amputation. But the need for it was often debatable; and to amputate or not to amputate became the great surgical controversy of the war, a controversy in which Mary played a minor part.[34]

Only a few peripheral incidents relating to Mary's experience at Fredericksburg have survived. Shortly after the battle she moved north to the Potomac at Aquia Creek, where injured men were being loaded aboard transports for Washington. She noticed that army ambulance corps were carrying the patients down the slope on their litters with their heads in front and often below the level of their feet. To prevent unnecessary suffering from such carelessness, she stopped the line, and ordered the carriers to turn about and bear the injured feet first.

On the transport she comforted a drummer boy who had lost both feet and was approaching death. Learning that he was the only child of a widow, who had recently arrived in Washington to see him, Mary searched until she found her to break the sad news. Finding that the widow had no means of support, she convinced her to remain in the city and work for the welfare of the soldiers. She eventually procured a position for her in an asylum for the war-shocked and insane.

During the early months of 1863 Mary again found time to attend to her columns in the *Sibyl*. One in March satirized women in Washington who attempted to move about the muddy city in hoops and crinoline. She had watched the expressions of disapproval on the faces of gentlemen, when ladies bespattered with mud attempted to guide their hoops into the streetcars, and had overheard a conductor, whose shoes and broadcloth were begrimed from rubbing against women's skirts, declare that he wished that all women would adopt sensible clothes such as she (Mary) was wearing.[15]

One of her more dubious contributions was an essay on "Woman's Mind," in which she maintained that the feminine mind was "capable of the profoundest reasoning, and reaches all of its conclusions through reasoning." As partial justification for this startling assertion, she cited her own mental powers. "I have a woman's mind, and know that all of my conclusions are obtained through the reasoning powers and not through instinct. Let no man dare say that woman jumps at conclusions through instinct, for no man is capable of fathoming a woman's mind. A woman reasons by telegraph, and his stage-coach reasoning cannot keep pace with hers. Woman's mind is an emanation from Deity, and man's mind is very probably emanated from the same source, and the difference in the minds of the sexes is owing in part to the roughness of the clay that is the message-bearer or soul-clogger of the mind[!]"[16]

An article extoling the "unheralded faithfulness" of women working for the soldiers, and a second, on positions which women of right ought to occupy, were less theoretical and more timely. She predicted that the war would inevitably bring greater freedoms for women, but warned that the ordeal would be prolonged unless enlightened leadership permitted greater utilization of female talents. Thinking of her own limited role, she complained, "I confess myself unable to see how respectable men can allow a laundress to go with their regiment, and shake their wise heads at the respectability of an educated lady acting as surgeon."[17]

Mary's letters to the *Sibyl* maintained her position of leadership in the dress-reform movement in New York State despite her prolonged absence. At the annual convention of the reform-dress society at Rochester in March, 1863, she was elected sixth vice-president on a list of thirteen.

At the start of the spring campaigns Mary was in Washington, where she recorded her impressions of the arrival of Confederate prisoners taken at Chancellorsville. An interested spectator, also, was President Lincoln.

"Father Abraham," she noted, waited at the Sixth Street Wharf for signs of Hooker's success. The day was warm, and large drops of perspiration rolled down his "careworn cheeks." The prisoners were fatigued and bedraggled. "Some had a piece of ingrain carpet for a blanket, some had no hats, but wore a turban made of a handkerchief, while those who had hats or caps looked as though they had served them since 1860; some had no shoes or stockings; some no coats, and nothing but a woolen shirt about their waists. Their clothing was of all colors, variegated with the sacred soil." Many looked pale and undernourished, "but when Secesh sympathizers took fruits and refreshments to them, the Provost Marshal would not allow such a demonstration."[18]

But the prisoners were not the only curiosity in Washington. Mary's unique appearance, personality, and varied activities caught the imagination of a reporter for the New York *Tribune,* and he featured her in the columns of his paper. It is the most colorful portrayal of her wartime operations:

> Among the unmarshalled host of camp-followers of the army, not the least noteworthy personage is Miss Mary E. Walker, or "Dr. Walker" as she is usually styled. . . . She is a native of New York, has received a regular medical education, and believes her sex ought not to disqualify her for the performance of deeds of mercy to the suffering heroes of the Republic. Dressed in male habiliments, with the exception of a girlish-looking straw hat, decked off with an ostrich feather, with a petite figure and feminine features, the *tout ensemble* is quite engaging. Her reputation is unsullied, and she carries herself amid the camp with a jaunty air of dignity well calculated to receive the sincere respect of the soldiers. . . . She can amputate a limb with the skill of an old surgeon, and administer medicine equally as well. Strange to say that, although she has frequently applied for a permanent position in the medical corps, she has never been formally assigned to any particular duty. . . . She is at present temporarily attached to the Sanitation Commission, whose headquarters are at the Lacey House opposite Fredericksburg.

39

We will add that the lady referred to is exceedingly popular among the soldiers in the hospitals, and is undoubtedly doing much good.[19]

While the *Tribune* correspondent doubtless exaggerated Mary's contributions with the scalpel, his observation that she was "undoubtedly doing much good," seems justified. Lacking an official assignment, she had, nevertheless, found opportunities to serve. That no task was too small is suggested by a favor which she rendered in the spring of 1863. Knowing that Oswego families were concerned about their sons and husbands who were sick and wounded, and would be desirous of learning where they were, she copied the names of those who had been committed to the hospitals in the Washington area from the medical director's records, and forwarded the list to the local press—fifty seven names in some twenty hospitals. It was a task which was truly beyond the line of duty.[20]

CHAPTER IV

ASSISTANT SURGEON AND A CONGRESSIONAL MEDAL OF HONOR

Mary's experiences during the next year read like a cloak-and-dagger thriller. She left Washington for the Tennessee front in the autumn of 1863, and arrived at Chattanooga as the casualties from Chickamauga were streaming into the city, just after September 19-20. The city was a vast hospital, where again an undermanned medical staff struggled desperately to save lives and alleviate suffering. Mary's services at this juncture appear to have caught the attention of General George H. Thomas. And when the assistant surgeon of the Fifty-second Ohio Infantry, stationed at Gordon's Mills southeast of Chattanooga, died unexpectedly, she was ordered to report to the commanding officer of the regiment, Colonel Dan McCook, as the surgeon's replacement. An unidentified clipping editorialized, "The young lady is very pretty and is said to thoroughly understand her profession. We imagine that the bitter pills which the sick of Col. McCook's brigade take hereafter, will be deprived of a great proportion of their nausea by the fair hands which prescribed them."

But the medical staff of the Army of the Cumberland did not see the joke. Dr. Perin, its Medical Director, was resolved that the sick and wounded should not be entrusted to such a "medical monstrosity," and ordered a medical board to examine her qualifications. There is little doubt that the board was ready to condemn her, whatever the evidence, and the most charitable interpretation of their action is that they might have heard what they came prepared to hear. In any event, after meeting with Mary, the board found her so inadequate "as to render it doubtful whether she has pursued the study of medicine." It admitted that she knew something of obstetrics [scarcely an endorsement for army duty], but that her knowledge of diseases and remedies was "not much greater than most house wives."[1]

Several years later, when Mary was in England, a reporter

41

quizzed her regarding this examination. She denied that she had ever appeared before such a board. "I was not in Georgia, Tennessee or Kentucky at the time stated," she said, "and was never examined by Medical Director Perin, and never saw him; nor was I ever examined by any board that he had appointed."[2]

Since she could not have forgotten such a humiliating experience, her denial appears to have been an attempt to dodge what she undoubtedly considered a kangaroo court.

Despite the unfavorable report, Mary remained at her post, wielding her new-found authority with such vigor that she seems to have repelled at least some of her patients. The regimental historian, the Reverend Nixon B. Stewart, who may not have been an impartial witness, wrote that the men seemed to hate her. "She began to practice in her profession among the citizens in the surrounding country. Every day she would pass out of the picket line, attending the sick. . . . Many of the boys believed her to be a spy."[3]

In explanation of his observation, it should be noted that the regiment was in winter quarters at this time, and presumably in good health, and Mary may have attended noncombatants in addition to her regimental duties, and not in lieu of them. In any event, at the end of the war Mary traveled hundreds of miles to revisit her old comrades in the Ohio 52nd.

The Reverend Stewart's observation that Mary passed through the picket line daily to attend the sick was no exaggeration. She roamed far and wide on horseback to make her calls and observe at first hand a sector of the war-weary South. She found families in which all of the men had gone off to war, including the sixteen-year-olds. Those who remained sometimes hid in swamps and thickets to avoid impressment. She found many in poverty and lacking basic necessities. They were gravely in need of physicians and medical supplies, and Mary seems to have dipped liberally into army stores to mitigate their wants.

In retrospect, it was one of her most gratifying war experiences. She recalled the warmth of her reception, once the initial misgivings stemming from her identification as a Yankee and her unladylike costume were broken down. She sometimes remained overnight, sleeping in their beds.

In her reminiscences, Mary recalled an incident which reflects both the hospitality and the doubts created by her masculine attire. While caring for a patient in a Tennessee home, she remained for the night, and slept with a daughter in an unconnected wing of the house. When she called again, the lady of the house offered her the same room, but would not permit her daughter to go with her, because, she said, people in the neighborhood alleged that she was a man. Not wishing to sleep alone in such isolated quarters, Mary requested that the mother and daughter go into a bedroom with her. She unbraided her hair, and asked the former to pull it, so that she might see if it were real. She did so, easily at first, but finally with a tug. She was convinced, and the daughter accompanied Mary to the bedroom as before.

Years later, in answer to a query regarding the service which had won for her a Congressional Medal of Honor, she pointed to her work with the destitute civilians near Chattanooga. "The special valor," she noted, "was for going into the enemy's ground, when the inhabitants were suffering for professional service, and sent to our lines to beg assistance; and no man surgeon was willing to respond for fear of being taken prisoner; and by my doing so the people were won over to the Union."[4]

One short news item made the rounds during her residence at the regimental headquarters at Gordon's Mills. Acknowledging that the report was unconfirmed, it noted that Mary had arrived at Colonel McCook's headquarters at night and, lacking accommodations for her, he had turned over his tent to her. Later, an officer, not knowing of the switch in quarters, entered McCook's tent with a dispatch, and tugged at what he thought was the colonel's leg to rouse him. A shriek from Mary sent him reeling from the tent in utter confusion.[5]

Mary is responsible for the preservation of several additional incidents at the headquarters here. With a review scheduled one day, Colonel McCook was called away. Before leaving he asked Mary to exchange her green sash for a red one, and to review the regiment for him. It was a thrilling experience to ride down the lines on horseback with an orderly at either side.

Again, while beyond the lines one day, without arms or escort, Mary encountered two men as they came from an old barn. They ordered her to halt, and asked her where she was going, and did she have revolvers in her saddle bags. She replied that she was on her way to see patients, and offered to show them her surgical

43

instruments as proof. The leader of the two shrugged off her suggestion and told her to go on. She did so, with a premonition that she had seen his face before. Later, when she chanced to view a picture of Champ Ferguson, the notorious Confederate guerrilla, she was convinced that he was the mysterious stranger who had intercepted her on that lonely road.[6]

On April 10, 1864, while on an expedition, Mary took the wrong road, and encountered a sentry of the enemy. According to her version of the incident, the sentry presented his rifle and ordered her to stop. She threw up her hands and declared herself unarmed. The sentry took her into custody as a prisoner of war.

The details of her captivity, with several exceptions, must be taken from speeches which Mary delivered a few years later, and which were recorded in the newspapers, particularly English publications.

She was confined in a cabin overnight, and delivered on the following day to General D. H. Hill, and by him to General Johnston. She remained at the latter's headquarters for a week. By being cooperative and friendly she was permitted to treat a limited number of patients. Callers included several medical officers, who, she soon discovered, were questioning her to ascertain whether a woman was really qualified to be a physician. She was next taken to Dalton, Georgia, for rail transportation to Richmond, about 700 miles distant. The trip required a week. News that a Yankee lady physician in bloomers was aboard preceded the train via telegraph, and the curious turned out at the various stops. At one point a physician feigned illness to test her medical knowledge, but she quickly discovered the ruse. Despite orders to keep her under strict surveillance, she persuaded her guards to take her from the car to visit a theater; she paid the price of admission for seven guards.

They finally reached Richmond, where she was confined in Castle Thunder, a political prison on Cary Street. The building had previously been used as a tobacco warehouse. As she entered, there was a cry of "fresh fish," which she soon discovered did not refer to the menu, but to herself, a scarcely flattering sobriquet given to new arrivals. She found the prison to be dirty, and her mattress infested with vermin. There were also vermin of a larger species which raced along the floors, particularly during the hours before dawn, making sleep impossible.[7]

But the atmosphere did not undermine her morale. Writing to her parents shortly after her arrival, she reassured them that she was comfortable. "I hope you are not grieving about me because I am a prisoner of war. I am living in a three-story brick 'castle' with plenty to eat, and a clean bed to sleep in. I have a room-mate, a young lady about twenty years of age from near Corinth, Mississippi. . . . The officers are gentlemanly and kind, and it will not be long before I am exchanged."[8]

In an article to the *National Republican* after her release, she described the prison fare, "as good, as abundant, as various as could be afforded." It consisted largely of corn bread, rice, peas and bacon. Women were served the same rations as men, and she had the part-time services of a female servant to help prepare her food. Outside in Richmond, she reported, food was bringing fantastic prices, and "there were hundreds in the city that would be glad to be as well provided as we were." Some of the Rebel soldiers, she noted, shared their rations with the starving populace.[9]

Once, she had tired of corn bread, and had reported that she could not swallow another mouthful. To her surprise, a few days later prisoners began to receive wheat bread. She had also insisted that the prisoners should receive more fresh vegetables, such as cabbage, because of their iron content. A short time thereafter, cabbage appeared on the menu as often as three or four times weekly.. She disclaimed any credit for these improvements. With an obvious attempt at levity she closed with an offer of thanks to Jefferson Davis for her entertainment at the "Hotel de Castle Thunder."[10]

When Mary related her prison experiences later in lectures, she was far more critical of the prison fare. The meals were scanty, and limited to two per day. She declared that a typical meal consisted of either a small slice of bread and a piece of bacon, or two spoonsful of rice or peas stirred in a pint of hot water taken from the river. Her misery grew with the telling!

Among the privations none was more enervating than the heat and foul air in the reconverted warehouse during the humid summer months. Two eyewitnesses saw her as she sought relief from her fetid quarters. A fellow prisoner once observed her at an open window where she was fanning herself with one hand and holding an American flag in the other. On another occasion, "a nondescript shape" was spied upon a balcony of the prison by three cavalrymen as they marched into Richmond as prisoners of war. "She made us a salutation and, with some misgivings, we gravely returned it. It was Dr. Mary Walker."[11]

The people of Richmond treated Mary as a curiosity, and their impressions sometimes got into print. The *Richmond Examiner*, for example, reported that she did not like her quarters and wished to go home. "She spent her confinement, not in reading medical works on saw bones and the treatment of camp itch," it continued, "but devouring all the novel nonsense and trash she can get hold of with a negro character in them." It noted that her costume was the bloomer style, and that she would not substitute it for one "more becoming to her sex."[12]

Mary recorded a visit by a prison doctor for the purpose of vaccinating her against smallpox. Though she never seems to have opposed vaccination, per se, she believed that it frequently caused serious complications, and she was in no mood to submit to it. Even if she had wavered, a pipe extending from the physician's mouth would have steeled her against it. She played for time, drawing him into a discussion of the merits of vaccination. At length, when he persisted, she seized her medicine case and declared that, if she thought it would be efficacious, she would do the job herself. The physician finally withdrew, his mission unaccomplished.[13]

Mary unleashed a barrage of letters from Castle Thunder in quest of a release. But weeks passed without action. She later told of an interview with the Provost Marshal, who declared that he might be "sympathetic" toward her, if she would dress like other ladies. "But she could not lose her self-respect even at the prospect of being freed. She told him that women had no more right to be dictated to by men than men had to be dictated to by women; that nine-tenths of women consumed half their energies by carrying about a bundle of clothes which not only weakened them, but were always in other people's way." She continued her "lecture" until the Provost Marshal terminated the interview.[14]

She was released from her imprisonment on August 12, 1864. With several hundred other prisoners she was placed aboard the flag-of-truce steamer *New York* which passed down the James River to Fortress Monroe at Hampton Roads inside Union lines. She declared later that the realization that she was free, coming

46

to her as the ship entered Union waters, was overpowering. The starry banner seemed too sacred for her touch. And almost as satisfying as freedom itself was the recognition which it implied; for she was exchanged as a surgeon for a Southern officer with the rank of major and, as she expressed it, one who was "six feet tall." She never forgot, or permitted others to forget it.[15]

She returned to Washington for a few weeks to recuperate from her ordeal, and then headed for the West. The press reported that she passed through Louisville and Nashville en route to Sherman's front near Atlanta. She planned "to visit General McCook and her old brigade, settle her business, obtain her trunk and bid adieu to the army. She will make a tour through the states, and lecture on her experience down in Dixie."[16]

She lost little time on this venture, for she was in Oswego before election day in November, the toast of the Republicans who were working desperately to re-elect Lincoln and upset Governor Horatio Seymour, the Democratic incumbent in New York. At a giant rally in Doolittle Hall on October 24 she related her adventures behind Rebel lines. Unfortunately, the local Republican paper did not record the details. She cleverly capitalized upon the opportunity, however, to promote Lincoln's candidacy, charging that every Rebel, with whom she talked in Richmond, favored the election of General McClellan, Lincoln's Democratic opponent. She also alleged that her exchange had been delayed even though the War Department had offered an officer of equal rank. And, needing a ruse to expedite her release, she had prepared some thirty pages of manuscript highly laudatory of McClellan, which she purported to be an electioneering address. Persuaded that its delivery in the North would materially assist "little Mac," the Rebels had ordered her exchange. Oswego Republicans loved the story; the reaction of the Democrats needs no elaboration.[17]

She closed her address with a tribute to Lincoln: "I do believe that if the worst Copperhead could but see the President after 'Cabinet Meeting,' just catch one glance at his careworn face, and feel that his great heart was constantly throbbing for the best interests of the most envied of countries in the World, they would forgive everything they censure him for, and put their shoulders to the wheel of the mammoth Republican car, instead of blocking the same."

Mary subsequently claimed that she had also campaigned from Washington to Atlanta (via Louisville) for Lincoln, laboring every evening, running risks in Louisville from the hostile populace, sustaining the Administration in public and private, and "saying things that few men would dare utter there." She also boasted that she had preached Lincoln's re-election before army audiences, "10,000 at a time."[18] It might be added that, consistent with her politics after the war, Mary's focus was upon the Union Party and the re-election of Lincoln, not the triumph of the Republican Party per se.

During the months after her initial rejection for an appointment as surgeon Mary continued to agitate for such a position, with of course the status and emolument commensurate with it. But each new approach produced a new rebuff, and only her phenomenal tenacity sustained her. In January, 1864, having exhausted, it seems all other channels, she appealed directly to President Lincoln. She advised him of her services while acting as an Assistant Surgeon in the hospitals and on the battlefield, and of her rejection for a commission solely on account of her sex. "The undersigned," she continued, "asks to be assigned to duty at Douglas Hospital, in the female ward, as there can not possibly be any objection urged on account of her sex, but she would much prefer to have an extra surgeon's commission with orders to go whenever and wherever there is a battle that she may render aid in the field hospitals, where her energy, enthusiasm, professional abilities and patriotism will be of the greatest service in inspiring the true soldier never to yield to traitors, and in attending the wounded brave. She will not shrink from duties under shot and shells, believing that her life is of no value in the country's greatest peril if by its loss the interests of future generations shall be promoted." Mary's scheme of a roving assignment would appear to be the Utopia military personnel have dreamed of for centuries!

While it is doubtful whether Lincoln received many applications less modest than this, he had few which were more eloquent.

In less than a week Mary had a reply; it was another rejection. Writing in his own hand at the bottom of Mary's letter, Lincoln observed:

The Medical Department of the Army is an organized system in the hands of men supposed to be learned in that profession, and I am sure it would injure the service for me, with strong hand, to thrust among them anyone, male or female, against their consent. If they are willing for Dr. Mary Walker to have charge of a female ward, if there be one, I also am willing, but I am sure controversy on the subject will not subserve the public interest.

A. Lincoln
Jan. 16, 1864[19]

But it turned out that even the President's decision was not the last word, for in September, 1864, she received the sum of $432.36 for services as contract physician from March 11, 1864, to August 23, 1864.[20] Ironically, she had spent more than four of these five months as a prisoner of war.

It is obvious that the Medical Department did not initiate this windfall. Most responsible for it was Colonel McCook of the Ohio 52nd, who had assigned duties to Mary, despite the opposition of the medical staff. McCook's recommendation, accompanied by General George H. Thomas' favorable endorsement, seems to have been decisive. Perhaps the latter's newly won fame as the Rock of Chickamauga may have tipped the balance.

A few weeks later Mary's good fortunes skyrocketed, when on October 5 she was awarded a contract as Acting Assistant Surgeon, United States Army, with a salary of $100 a month.[21] As a *female* Assistant Surgeon she was unique in the annals of the American Army. She remained on duty in this capacity until the close of the war.

Her initial assignment, dated September 22, 1864, was at Louisville, Kentucky, where she was named Surgeon in the Women's Prison Hospital. It was a far cry from her more glamorous duties with the soldiers, and she was soon out of sympathy with what she considered to be the ungrateful demands of her patients.

"They [the prisoners] have the best coffee, soup, potatoes, fresh beef (over half a pound at each plate) and the very best bread," she noted with unfeigned disapproval. "Could I have had the quality and quantity in a week, while a prisoner in Richmond, that each one of these prisoners consumes in a day, I could

49

not have complained of the 'bill of fare.'" On Thanksgiving Day, she noted, they had an excellent dinner, provided by a "pretended" Union woman: turkey, chicken, celery, pies, and cakes. She regretted that it was not being served to the soldiers.[22]

To make her situation even less congenial, she found that the officers and hospital attendants were critical of her leniency toward the prisoners. In a letter to her superior in command, Mary justified her regulations and elaborated upon her problems:

> She would tolerate no Rebel songs or disloyal talk; no familiarity between guards, male cooks, and prisoners, and no profanity. She required that visitors be watched carefully, and that all letters passed to the prisoners be examined. She placed offenders in confinement, and on one occasion applied handcuffs. She defended the food, charging that complaints stemmed from her replacement of male cooks with females rather than the quality of the food.[23]

Mary persevered at her post for six months. Then, finding that she pleased neither friend nor foe, she requested a transfer to the fighting front. She was relieved from her onerous assignment on March 22, 1865. Later, she had the satisfaction of a favorable report from her medical director, Dr. Edward Phelps, who noted that in performing the complicated duties of her office, she had shown "the same active, energetic, and perservering spirit which had enabled her to render even more services to her country than many of our efficient officers bearing full commissions."[24] Mary also retained the loyalty and confidence of her orderly at Louisville, who testified that she was always kind and attentive to both prisoners and guards. Unfortunately, he continued, her consideration for the former displeased some Union people.[25]

Incidentally, Mary's young nephew, Charles Griswold of Oswego, just sixteen, accompanied her to Louisville to serve as her orderly. According to family tradition he was taken ill only a few weeks after his arrival and was sent home.

From Louisville Mary was ordered to Nashville, to report to the Medical Director of the Department of the Cumberland. Here she was placed in charge of an orphan asylum at Clarksville, and made responsible, also, for refugee families housed in the neighborhood.

She was at Clarksville during the closing scenes of the war, and on Easter Sunday, a week after Lee's surrender to Grant and two days after Lincoln's assassination, became involved in an explosive issue. Evidence in the affair is limited to two letters in the *Louisville Journal*. The first, signed "Episcopalian," was highly critical of Mary's behavior at the services of the Episcopal Church in Clarksville, and the second was Mary's explanation and defense of her conduct.

According to Mary's critic, a woman physician, known as Dr. Walker, attended the morning service, and was seated at the front of the crowded sanctuary. She at once "attracted the general attention of the congregation, owing to the peculiarity of her dress. She wore the Federal Uniform, modified only by a short tunic above the knee, and cavalry boots, with shoulder straps showing her to rank as a Major." From her place the Doctor observed an arrangement of flowers in the baptismal font, a circle of white Easter lilies with a single red geranium at its center. Though the colors spelled no political significance the lady medic assumed that the red and white were designed to glorify the fallen Confederacy. When the *Te Deum Laudamus* was begun she stepped forward to the font, and pinned a piece of blue ribbon to the lilies, meanwhile grimacing defiantly at the rector. A short time later he removed the ribbon and continued the service.

The offensive doctor was again present at the evening service. According to her critic she was now wearing pistols. She also carried a small American flag tied with crepe, and a small bouquet bound with the same. She proceeded to the front of the auditorium, and placed the flag on the chancel rail so that it leaned against the font, and dropped the bouquet at its side.

While the offering was being taken the minister set the flag and bouquet to one side, whereupon the oddly dressed incendiary indignantly replaced them. The atmosphere was charged.

Every soldier was on the alert—as far as the soldiers are concerned, if they really thought the red was placed in the Church from any political move, we can not censure them for resenting it, particularly at this time—but we do censure her who incited such feelings. If the flowers were typical of disloyalty, to the Colonel commanding belonged the right to remove or have them removed.

We do not know whether Major Walker considers
herself a lady or not. Judging from her costume we suppose not, and certainly no gentleman would so dese-
crate the House of God. We will simply call her Neutral
Major."[26]

Mary's defense was a vigorous counter-offensive. No one but a
coward would make such a personal attack and not sign his
name. She carried no pistols; she wore no cavalry boots; nor had
she brought the controversial bouquet. She declared that she had
been shocked by the attitude of the minister and the audience on
that, the first Sunday after the death of President Lincoln. She
also alleged that the rector, while complaining of the incident to
the commandant, had said that there were no blue flowers in
bloom at that time. And to prove her point that the omission was
deliberate, she had gathered a bouquet of blue violets growing
nearby, and presented them to the commandant.[27]

While it was a tempest in a teapot, it was a prelude to the
bitterness, which was to follow. Were the Rebels contrite, or were
they simply awaiting an opportunity to rise again?

The affair scarcely suggests an attitude of sympathy or understanding on Mary's part for Southerners in their most difficult
hours.

Shortly after this Easter Sunday embroglio Mary was ordered
to Washington, where her war service officially ended on June 15.

Three weeks after her discharge, Mary was in Richmond with
a delegation of Northerners to celebrate the Fourth of July with
their former enemies. While many residents of the former Confederate Capital took advantage of the holiday to escape the
dust and heat of the city and seek a respite on the river or in the
parks, a crowd gathered in Capitol Square just after 10 A.M. for
the scheduled festivities. Spectators soon discovered that the
celebrants were exclusively Yankee. Under a broiling sun the
Rev. Dr. Stockwood of Massachusetts offered a short opening
prayer, and the brass band of the 39th Illinois Regiment contributed a national air.

The stage was now set for the principal attraction. Dr. Mary
Walker, resplendent in her surgeon's uniform, mounted the steps
of the Capitol, paused for the undivided attention of the audience and began to read:

When, in the course of human events, it becomes necessary for one people to dissolve the political bands which have connected them with another, and to assume, among the powers of the earth, the separate and equal station to which the laws of nature and of nature's God entitle them. . . .

She stopped only when she had finished reading Jefferson's immortal Declaration of Independence. After she stepped down there were several speeches and a benediction. The firing of a salute by the Illinois troops brought the celebration to a close. For Mary it was a triumphant return to the scene of her incarceration; it may have been, also, her last appearance in army blues.

Seven months later Congress and the President provided a more formal and climactic military farewell, when on January 24, 1866, she received from President Johnson the Congressional Medal of Honor for Meritorious Service, dated November 11, 1865.

It read:

Executive Office

Whereas it appears from official reports that Dr. Mary E. Walker, a graduate of medicine, "has rendered valuable service to the Government, and her efforts have been earnest and untiring in a variety of ways," and that she was assigned to duty and served as an assistant surgeon in charge of female prisoners at Louisville, Ky., upon the recommendation of Major-Generals Sherman and Thomas, and faithfully served as contract surgeon in the service of the United States, and has devoted herself with much patriotic zeal to the sick and wounded soldiers, both in the field and hospitals, to the detriment of her own health, and has endured hardships as a prisoner of war four months in a southern prison while acting as contract surgeon; and

Whereas by reason of her not being a commissioned officer in the military service a brevet or honorary rank can not, under existing laws, be conferred upon her; and

Whereas in the opinion of the President an honorable recognition of her services and sufferings should be made;

It is ordered. That a testimonial thereof shall be hereby made and given to the said Dr. Mary E. Walker, and that the usual medal of honor for meritorious services be given her.

Given under my hand in the city of Washington, D.C. this 11th day of November, A.D. 1865.

Andrew Johnson, *President*

By the President:

Edwin M. Stanton, *Secretary of War*[28]

Mary wore the medal, sometimes flanked by several others, from that day forward—her most cherished possession. In 1907 she received a replacement for the original with a slightly modified design. She wore both of them!

It seems ironic that in 1917, some fifty years later, the Board of Medal Awards, while reviewing the merits of the Civil War awards, should have ruled Mary's as unwarranted. Now eighty-five, the old soldier went down fighting. She reviewed the highlights of her career for the board. The medal was for valor; had she not earned it? It had been given to her legally and properly, had it not? She would go on wearing both medals. "One of them I will wear every day, and the other I will wear on occasions." The board would not reconsider. There was nothing in the records, it insisted, to show the specific act or acts upon which the decoration was awarded.[29]

The blow may well have hastened her death two years later. True to her word, she retained the medals to the end.

CHAPTER V

THOSE CONTROVERSIAL PANTALOONS

While the Civil War years were without doubt the most colorful of Mary's long life, they were in reality a mere introduction to a full half-century of restless striving for lost causes. Times changed, as the nineteenth century yielded to the twentieth, but the young militant simply became the old militant, fighting the same battles with the same weapons.

After Appomattox many veterans exchanged their rifles for the tools which they had dropped in 1861, but for Mary the transition was more complicated. True, she went through the motions of going back to the practice of medicine. But she remained in Washington, and was soon taking time from her practice, which appears to have been quite modest, to promote social issues.

Her attention was first drawn to the plight of the hundreds of women who had served as nurses during the war. It seemed logical that they should receive pensions and other benefits available to male veterans. Mary took their cause to the press, citing cases of distress, some of them war sustained. She indicated that the twenty dollars a month which was sought was a "pitiable sum" for women who had "worn out their lives in our hospitals."[1]

Indicative of broader feminist goals is a petition drafted in Mary's hand, which adds to the usual request for pensions the plea that "the right of the franchise shall not be denied to any of the women citizens of the United States or Territories, who labored ninety days in the hospitals for the sick or wounded of the late war."[2]

Mary and her associates were instrumental in having bills for the relief of nurses introduced in Congress, only to see them die in committee.

Her failures had significance for her future, however, in that they initiated a practice of going to Washington, to Congress, the White House, or any other agency which might be used to promote woman's rights. Through the years she made dozens of trips and spent countless hours in interviews and committee rooms in quest of them, until she was identified on sight by thousands of Washingtonians from the President down. It also served to convince her that the Civil War had somehow won political rights for women, which were guaranteed by the Declaration of Independence and the Constitution, but never exercised, and that women might vote and hold office simply by demanding it with such force that reluctant males could not resist the pressure.

During these months just after the war Mary also responded to an appeal from Dr. Lydia Sayer Hasbrouck to resume her leadership in the dress reform movement.

"Where in the name of common sense are you to be found," the former editor of the *Sibyl* inquired. "We see your name here, there and some where, but not one line from you this long time.

"Now that you have done your work in the army, we want you North. We want to go to work in earnest upon the question of woman's right to suffrage and the dress question.

"We want to put lecturers into the field, and we want you to help us as Sergeant Major to martialize our forces."[3]

Mary did not need the invitation to continue the crusade for dress reform, but it was, nevertheless, a reassuring call to action. She proved her dedication to it in New York in June, 1866, in a fashion which attracted nation-wide publicity to herself and to dress reform.

While she was shopping in a millinery store on Canal Street, near Broadway, her bizarre costume attracted a crowd of onlookers, principally women and children. Fearful that Mary was in danger, the operator of the store called a policeman, and asked him to escort her home. When he asked Mary for her address, he received the startling reply that it was "anywhere the Stars and Stripes fly." He led her through the assemblage, with Mary protesting that she needed no protection, and then ordered her to accompany him to the precinct police station. She did so under protest. The two were followed by a goodly number of the curious multitude. At the police station Mary at first refused to divulge her name or address on the ground that her detention was unwarranted. She relented, however, when the sergeant threatened to lock her up, and invited the patrolman to check her name on her medal. When he showed no inclination to do so, she came forward to permit a better inspection of it. She also took the precaution of writing down the number on the sergeant's badge, for further reference. When he asked Mary whether she could read and write, she indignantly shot back, "I don't know a letter of the alphabet." At this point the sergeant seems to have reached the point of diminishing returns, and told the policeman to see her through the crowd. She hastened to reject the offer. "When I wish the protection of a policeman," she quipped, "I will ask an intelligent one."[4]

She had no intention of dropping the matter here, however, since it might serve as a test case to guarantee freedom from arbitrary arrest in the future. She at once filed charges of improper conduct against the patrolman who had taken her to court.

The case came before Police Commissioner Thomas C. Acton a few days later. A large audience, including a sprinkling of reporters, was on hand. It was a perfect sounding board, and she made the most of her opportunity.

Her very attire was a testimonial to her cause: "The suit was of fine black broadcloth, and consisted of a dress or gown gathered at the waist in the manner of ordinary dresses, and a skirt reaching thence a little below the knee. Under this was worn pantaloons of the same material, loosely fitting the limbs, and open at the feet as in male attire. The whole appearance of the dress was very suggestive of convenience, ease of motion and personal neatness. The wearer had the air of a lady with perhaps a slight tinge of (feminine) smartness and loquacity."

Paying no attention to the policeman involved, Mary launched into a defence of the dress reform. She had been coming to New York, she declared, for seven or eight years in the bloomer type of dress, and had always been treated with respect by the police. On one occasion, she had been accompanied by four or five others similarly dressed.

They wore the reform dress because they found long dresses uncomfortable and inconvenient. It was impossible to go up and down stairs without wiping the filth from them. In the streets their dresses became so begrimed that they had to change them every time they went out. They deemed it impossible to wear hoops in the street when the wind blew, and avoid exposing the limbs. Aside from the inconvenience and immodesty of women's clothes, "we could not go up into Bunker Hill Monument or the dome of the Capitol with it." They wore the reform dress for its healthfulness. As a practicing physician she cited cases in which women had destroyed their health by trying to dress in fashion.

Finally, the bloomer dress was acceptable to men and women of the highest character and refinement. "I have been at the President's receptions many times, and have dined with officers of the government and their wives repeatedly. During the past winter I have boarded at a house where two Generals and their wives boarded and members of Congress, and have received all of the attention that ladies receive. I wish it understood that I wear this style of dress from the highest, the purest and the noblest principle. . . ."

Here the defendant's counsel interrupted to ask what Mary's remarks had to do with the case, but the Commissioner, who appeared to enjoy the proceedings, declared that she should state her position.

Encouraged to go on, Mary told her version of her involvement with the police. She minimized the size of the crowd and pointed out that, although the milliner had simply asked the officer to disperse the crowd, he had instead taken her to the police station.

When the defense counsel at last had an opportunity to speak, he argued that the wearing of men's clothes by a woman was an offense, and should she dress in such a manner as to attract a crowd and cause a public excitement, she should be arrested. The Commissioner interrupted to ask whether he held that Mary as dressed violated any law. He replied in the affirmative, defining it as a misdemeanor by law.

The defense then called upon the defendant, who insisted that he had not insulted or mistreated the plaintiff in any way.

Mary's attorney concluded by introducing a number of character references for his client, including President Johnson and other prominent personages. The Commissioner rejected them, however, as unnecessary.

He then announced his decision: "I consider, Madam, that you have as good a right to wear that clothing as I have to wear mine, and he [the defendant] has no more right to arrest you for it, than he has me. But if you were creating a disturbance, and there was a mob gathered there, he would be justified in removing you. He was fearful you would be insulted."

"Why didn't he let me go my own way?" Mary shot back.

Commissioner: "Because he knew the mob would follow you on the street and hoot after you."

Mary: "There was a street car I could have stepped into."

Commissioner: "You are smarter than most ladies in the City of New York. I would have had no hesitation in letting you go your own way . . . but he thought you a weak woman needing protection. [To the policeman] Let her go, she can take care of herself. Never arrest her again." [Loud laughter]

Thus the case ended: Mary's charges against the policeman were dismissed; but the Commissioner's defense of her right to wear pantaloons was interpreted to mean that police would not interfere in the future.

The newspapers featured the case, though their treatment of it varied from ridicule of Mary and dress reform to forthright support. More frequently they played up the comic aspects without editorializing. Some accounts were accompanied by cartoons. One, in two parts, first showed Mary in bloomer costume moving toward the police station with the heavy hand of a policeman on her shoulder, the caption reading "Immodesty under the law, Doctor Walker arrested for outraging the public's sense of propriety." The second cartoon depicted several ladies clad in hoop skirts, with their skirts pulled awry by the wind. The caption read: "Modesty according to law. But this pretty dear is not arrested because she does not violate the public's sense of propriety. Oh! No!"[5]

The *New York Times* called Mary's treatment unauthorized, and the *World* assumed that the Commissioner's decision would not permit any interference hereafter with women wearing breeches.

Mary seems to have had no further difficulties in New York, but she had to wage similar battles elsewhere.

Two weeks after this defense of bloomers Mary was in Syracuse to participate in a convention of the National Dress-Reform Association. Her personal battle for the cause at once propelled her to the forefront. In the absence of the president, she was chosen President Pro Tem, and later elected President for the ensuing year. She also delivered the principal address at the evening session which, to no one's surprise, was built around her New York story. She predicted that in less than ten years women would march side by side with men to the polls; and that women would hold many of the public offices. She also spoke at length upon her Civil War services, and finally got around to dress reform. For comedy relief she proposed that, since the public was agitated over the question of what to do with Jefferson Davis, she would answer that issue by dressing him in hoops and long-style skirts in keeping with the current fad, and require him to do the work of a woman managing a four-story house, and be made to go up and down the stairs seven times a day. Such punishment, she knew, would exceed any other that could be devised. Needless to say her audience was sympathetic, and her remarks were frequently interrupted by applause.

On the second day she again delivered an address, a shorter one devoted more specifically to dress reform. To demonstrate the attractiveness of the costume she brought models to the platform: a lady with a large frame; an elderly woman; a little girl; and for a fourth type, a slight figure, she presented herself! She proved to the satisfaction of her listeners that the dress reform was suited to all types and shapes of feminine humanity.

Prior to adjournment the convention adopted three resolutions: First, they thanked the Syracuse press for their kindness, courtesy and fairness; second, they commended Police Commissioner Acton, "for his decision in Dr. Walker's case in regard to the rights of women to walk the streets of New York clothed in a physiological manner." Third, they congratulated the press of New York City "for the able manner in which they have defended Dr. Mary E. Walker for advocating the inherent right of women to dress in a manner that comports with freedom of motion, health and morality."[6]

Needless to say it warmed the cockles of Mary's heart.

Chapter VI

AN ENGLISH CELEBRITY

In September of 1866 an unexpected opportunity came Mary's way in the guise of an invitation to serve as a delegate to a social science congress in Manchester, England. She appears to have entered upon the journey with several objectives in mind. She needed a rest. Her continuous round of activities had sapped her strength; she was thinner, and lines were beginning to mar the youthfulness of her face. A European tour would afford rest and relaxation, and enable her to see the historic spots of the old world. It would also be an opportunity to observe the progress of woman's rights in England, and to participate with English suffragists. Finally, she might visit English hospitals, and possibly observe surgery, a privilege frequently denied women in America.

She reached Liverpool a few weeks prior to the convention, with sufficient time to tour Scotland, and take a boat excursion along its west coast with a stop at historic Iona, famous for its sixth-century Christian monastery. Her unorthodox costume immediately caught the attention of the English press, and she continued to be newsworthy through the months of her residence there.

She appeared at the social science congress on October 8, and listened to the principal address, written by Madame Barbara Bodichon, the former Barbara Smith, a noted English feminist, but read by a Mr. Noel. At the top of a newspaper clipping of the speech, Mary wrote with unfeigned disgust, "Madame Bodichon presented a paper, but it was read by a man."[1] The address was an eloquent appeal for woman's suffrage. At its conclusion, the chairman called attention to the presence of "a distinguished foreigner, the innate modesty of whose sex prevents her from rising." He expressed the hope, however, that they might hear from her. Mary rose, the focus of all eyes. They saw:

61

A very slight figure . . . habited in a black surtout, fitting neatly to the body, and showing the width of waist, which is not merely of the orthodox pattern for young ladies, but "of the straitest sect." The skirt of the surcoat, in which is a side pocket, from which a white handkerchief peeps, falls considerably below the knee, and expanding from the waist in extinguisher fashion, it is closely buttoned throughout. The "continuation" [pants] are also of black, pretty full at the lower hem—in fact quite the opposite of peg top fashion; and a neat little pair of feet, which would be not quite unaristo-cratic in China, are fitted into an unexceptional pair of boots. The collar resembles, if not composed in fact, of white Japanned steel, with a clearer sheen than Glen-field starch, ending in a *quasi* tie, and forms a kind of slight cope to the dress, which fits close to the throat. The hair, in regard to which the lady graduate has not denuded herself of the "ornament of woman," is tied close up behind, and is shed in proper feminine division from crown to forehead. A very little black straw hat completes the attire.

Her features are thin and small, and she is yet young, although showing a few of those lines which years al-ways deepen. She is not pretty—not at least to admirers of plump and rosy faces—but in her manner she is en-gaging. . . . She will not break many hearts, but she may turn some heads.[2]

She turned heads that day, and held them as she spoke:

"Before all countries in the world," she declared, "Great Britain should give to women equal rights." While Her Noble Majesty [Queen Victoria] was the highest person in this great Kingdom, it was an insult to her not to put all of her sex on an equality with the rest of the community. England boasted of its Constitution and the United States of its freedom, yet women were denied the rights of the elective franchise. She predicted, however, that women would win the rights and privileges enjoyed by men within ten years. She denied the charge that women would not use their judgment, but would simply vote as their husbands did.

Honest differences between husbands and wives on political issues, she argued, would enhance rather than undermine family relations. The wisdom of a vote, she insisted, varied with intelligence, but had nothing to do with sex. She had observed that the most intelligent men were ready to accord to women what they deserved; the lowest class, on the other hand, strenuously opposed it. While woman was equal with man before the Deity, while at the last day of her life she had to walk into the presence of her Maker without a man to walk by her side to help her there . . . "was it right that in the few days of our stay here, man should trample his great foot on woman, because she was physically inferior?"[3]

There was little that was profound or original in her remarks, but the combination of her dress, personality, and speech captured the imagination of her audience. When the meeting adjourned, she was at once surrounded by questioners. To a Frenchman who expressed some negatives regarding her reform dress, she retorted that a thousand women in the United States now wore the costume, and that if Paris did not adopt it, America would take its place, and dictate styles to the world. To others she observed that the extreme in women's costumes—a general's wife who fastened 100 japonicas to her gown—would inevitably contribute to the reform. To still another circle she acknowledged that women, themselves, would require a great deal of persuasion before they would be willing to accept "physiological" attire.

A reporter referred to her as the "lion" or "lioness" of the occasion.[4]

Of more lasting significance than the flurry of attention at the congress were the friendships and the plethora of invitations which came her way: speaking engagements; visitations to hospitals; offers of hospitality from London, Bristol, Edinburgh, and elsewhere.

Among these friendships, that of the Rev. and Mrs. Charles W. Denison was perhaps the most valued. The Denisons were American residents in England, where Mr. Denison had a pastorate. They opened their home to her, and introduced her to their English acquaintances, a goodly number of whom were reform minded. They helped to plan her travels, and later accompanied her to Paris. Helpful, also, was James Edmunds, who was president and principal promoter of a female medical society.

63

Hopeful that Mary's presence would facilitate the acceptance of women in the medical profession, he arranged appearances for her before learned societies and special interest groups. Dozens of letters among the Walker manuscripts attest to the warm welcome offered by these and other English friends.[5]

One of Mary's first acceptances of hospitality was of that offered by the hospitals. She observed surgery at the Royal Infirmary at Glasgow and at the Manchester Royal Infirmary; in London she witnessed a series of operations at the Middlesex Hospital, including the reduction of a dislocated humerus, removal of a cancer at the base of the mouth, an operation for neurosis of the lower jaw, and an excision of epulis. She viewed surgery, also, at St. Bartholomew's Hospital in London. Here, Dr. Holmes Coate was especially helpful, making arrangements for her at St. Bartholomew's and accompanying her to others. He also offered his guidance to shield her from the lower classes of London, who, he feared, might molest her because of her male dress. Though Mary left no record of her impressions of English surgery, the contrasts between the techniques of a makeshift field hospital and the newest Continental practices could not have been unnoticed.

Meanwhile, she visited the tourist spots: Stratford-on-Avon, the London Bridge, the Tower of London and Westminster Abbey. She recorded her observations and, as in Washington, showed an interest in the minutiae about her: heights, breadths, building materials, Sir Walter Raleigh in the Tower, and many other details.

But sightseeing soon took second place to the lecture circuit, when on November 20, 1866, two months after her arrival, she made her debut at St. James's Hall in London.

The program read:

ST. JAMES'S HALL
Regent Street and Piccadilly
DR. MARY E.
W A L K E R
(from the United States of America)
Having been solicited by her friends during her stay
in this Country will give her first
L E C T U R E
In the Great St. James's Hall on

64

TUESDAY, NOVEMBER 20th, 1866
SUBJECT
The Experiences of a Female Physician in College,
in Private Practice, and in the Federal Army.
Doors open at 7.30; Lecture to commence at 8 o'clock
Precisely
Platform Chairs 7s.6d. Sofa Stalls (numbered and reserved), 5s. Reserved Seats, 3s. Balcony, 2s. Area and Galleries, 1s.⁶

The lecture was planned so as to evoke the broadest appeal. The American Civil War had stirred the British public as had few foreign affairs since Waterloo, and the similarity between Florence Nightingale in the Crimea and Mary in American field hospitals was expected to arouse interest. A young schoolgirl struggling to gain a foothold in a man's profession, a woman physician performing deeds of valor in the Union Army, and a suffragist clad in men's pants seemed to warrant a large hall and to invite long queues at the ticket office.

Still the performance was a gamble for Mary. It was one thing to be the toast of a dedicated band of reformers, but a very different matter to project her personality to the public at large, which would pay admission fees ranging from one shilling to seven shillings, six pence. All would be curious, many critical, and some openly hostile. Unfortunately, we can only speculate upon the misgivings which flashed before her mind as she faced the opening of the curtain.

The spacious hall was crowded as the opening hour approached. The galleries, filled with young men, including an undetermined number of medical students, were unusually noisy. Eight o'clock came and went, and the platform remained empty. Songs broke forth from the scattered sections of the galleries: "Glory Halleluiah" and "Slap Bang." As the demonstrations grew more hostile, there were shouts from occupants of the higher priced seats for silence, and calls for police. When a Bobby arrived, the din swelled rather than diminished. At length, the director, Mr. Nimmo, came to the rostrum and asked for order. The program was almost ready to start, he declared, but as the speaker was suffering from an indisposition which rendered her voice weak, she would be heard only if they would be attentive.

65

He appealed for a fair hearing, and the courtesy of silence. The hall quieted momentarily, but the din was again rising when Mary stepped forward. The audience hushed as they focused upon the slight, girlish figure, clad in the bloomer costume, which had already become her trademark in Great Britain. Only the blind could not have seen the sparkle of the Medal of Honor upon her dark tunic.

After first asking for forbearance, because of the weakness of her voice, she launched upon her life story. She told of reading in childhood from the works of a missionary who stressed the need for women skilled in medicine in heathen lands. She had resolved to become a physician, and practice in foreign parts, especially among members of her own sex. But she had faced formidable opposition, even ridicule. She had eventually been able to enter medical college, but difficulties continued to dog her path. She was denied admittance to a *post mortem* examination on the ground that the young woman must "have something soft in her head," but she persevered, reading human anatomy in her room by the hour when no one knew how she was employed. Some told her that it was a disgrace to her sex for a lady to practice medicine. This remark gave the scoffers in the gallery the opportunity they were waiting for. They cheered to show their agreement that it was a disgrace. But Mary would not be diverted. Continuing, she declared, "They asked me why I did not marry a doctor instead of setting up to be one myself." Laughter and shouts of "hear, hear!" exploded from the galleries.

After a pause for order, Mary continued her autobiography: she arose at four o'clock in the morning to pursue her studies; and her labors were at length crowned with success; she received her medical degree in the spring of 1855. She was prepared to go to the Crimea to administer professionally to the British soldiers, but the conclusion of the war denied her the opportunity.

Instead, she entered upon the practice of medicine in the United States. She soon discovered that some of her patients expected to pay less for her services than they would pay a man. The work of a woman, they argued, was always cheaper than that of a man. Mary's answer to them removed all doubts upon the matter. "My education had been quite as elaborate and occupied the same time, and cost as much. I can do the work I profess as well as any man. The obstacles I had to surmount were greater.

66

Therefore I am justified in charging not only as much, but more."
She quickly added, however, that she was content with "perfect
equality." Mary was interrupted here by the applause of the more
respectable portions of the audience. Continuing, she observed
that her practice expanded year after year. Her clients were
largely women and children, though the former occasionally requested that she attend their husbands. She had been asked why
people would patronize a woman doctor. Some came to her, she
declared, because they had confidence in her skill; others, because her office was convenient, and still others, because they
liked her personally. Some preferred her because she could get
dressed faster than a man! This remark created a near bedlam,
with raucous shouts sounding above the prolonged laughter.
Mary finally sat down and waited for the din to cease. She appeared unruffled.

When order was restored Mary described her search for an
attire suited to her profession. She dwelt at length upon the in-
conveniences of current styles in women's clothing, and the mala-
dies which they inflicted upon her sex. She regarded the weight
of long skirts, hanging from the waist rather than the shoulders,
as particularly deleterious. Victims, she predicted, would never
recover from their disabilities until they abandoned such clothing.
It was a recognized fact, she insisted, that long dresses were
killing their wearers.

Turning next to the American Civil War, she elaborated upon
her interpretation of the issues leading to the conflict. The audience soon tired of it, and there were shouts of "no politics." They
objected, also, to her repeated reference to the Confederates as
Rebels, a term considered altogether right and proper in those
parts of the United States north of the Mason and Dixon Line. It
is doubtful whether a briefing on the delicacy of this subject by
the United States Minister to the Court of St. James's, Charles
Francis Adams, would have softened Mary's analysis.

She eventually came to her personal experiences in the war,
and found the audience again attentive. She described her journeys with wounded soldiers, and touched briefly upon her captivity.

But again she digressed to the question of dress, and concluded by declaring that "whatever good she had been able to
do in the cause of suffering humanity, she attributed to the fact

of her having worn a healthful, convenient, and strength-saving costume."

When she stopped she received generous applause interspersed with scattered cheers. The large assemblage dispersed in a good-natured and orderly manner.[7]

The hour-and-a-half presentation had been a severe strain upon the ailing lecturer but, if she had any reservations about future performances, she did not express them. Instead, she was ready for the next engagement. She realized, however, that much would depend upon the reaction of the press, and she awaited the first issues of the London papers with trepidation.

By the following day the results were in: One after another the dailies gave her favorable reviews, and denounced the tenants of the galleries who had heckled her. She was referred to as "the distinguished American female surgeon"; her dress was "simple and becoming"; she made her dress "becoming by her peculiarly graceful form." Her elocution was "excellent," except for "occasional Americanisms," and her voice, "clear, musical, and penetrating," and "very distinct," but a "little theatrical at the start." There was a "calm and quiet dignity in her manner," and she spoke with "composure." The gallery contained a "mob of unruly boys, alleged, we hope falsely, to be medical students," who were "noisy and vulgar," and "even indecent," but she "cowed the gallery-full of stupid young gentlemen." Despite unseemly interruptions, "she did not once allow her temper to be ruffled, nor utter a reproach," and she "bore loud laughter with the most imperturbable good humor," and their "chaff with great equanimity." Again and again she paused, "resuming her lecture with patience and determination, which were legibly written on her high and clear forehead, and on her calm and pretty face."

A large majority of the audience were "deeply interested," and determined to give her a "fair hearing," and a "favorable reception." "She was well received, and worthy of a better reception."

"The most interesting portions related to her own experiences," but so much of it was taken up with "disquisitions on costume and the American War . . . the effect on the whole was rather disappointing." "The story of her life as a medical practitioner was amusing," and she was advised to dwell more on these details and "less on what is evidently still with her a womanly weakness, the subject of dress." It needed a little compression, but "expect it will be listened to with pleasure for successive audiences for many evenings to come." "She concluded amid cheers, which were also frequently bestowed during the course of her lecture."

Observed collectively, the reviews reveal an enthusiasm for Mary's personality, her manner of delivery, poise, and presence of mind. They also show a spirit of toleration toward her dress and her interpretation of the war. But they particularly enjoyed the story of her life, her trials in medical school, and as a pioneering woman physician; they also wished to hear more of her personal experiences in the war.[8]

The reviews stimulated interest, and she soon had a host of invitations for appearances.

The reviews were also helpful to Mary in making improvements in her presentation. Guided by their comments and the suggestions of her friends, she reorganized her materials into several lectures: One dealt with dress reform, and was planned for women's groups; a second, on temperance, was tailored to workingmen's clubs and temperance societies; a third, designed for mixed audiences, was a narration of her experiences as a young doctor in peace and war. However, there was a good deal of overlapping. Each of her lectures, whatever its title, inevitably became a plea for women's rights, and each was interspersed with her own experiences. The critics, with an assist from the galleries, suggested deletions so that she might avoid unpleasant interruptions from the audience. For example, she removed the boast of dressing faster than a man. Again, she struck out a reference to kissing the gravely wounded soldiers. Such a tender embrace seemed incongruous when told in pantaloons! However, the unpredictable was not eliminated, since Mary was quick to rise to the defense if challenged, and frequently strayed from her prepared notes. It added color and excitement to her presentation.

In addition to reviews and advertisements of her lectures, the English newspapers carried photographs and cartoons of Mary, some of them full length and as much as four columns in width, and she was news wherever she traveled. For example, a few days after her appearance at St. James's, it was reported that she planned to visit Guy's Hospital and witness surgery there. A crowd, including an unusual turnout of students and doctors, appeared at the gates to get a glimpse at the highly publicized female medic. But for reasons not explained, perhaps illness, Mary did not appear, "and the numerous assemblage dispersed, no doubt disappointed of an anticipated treat."[9]

At this time, also, the *London Anglo-American Times* published President Johnson's complete citation for her medal of honor, and observed that it was a distinction never before accorded to one of her sex. "Her strange adventures, thrilling experiences, important services and marvelous achievements exceed anything that modern romance or fiction has produced. Throughout her whole war life of four years she has persisted in wearing the 'short dress,' and by the indomitable energy of her will and inexhaustible resources of her 'strategy,' she has not only won the admiration of the military authorities of her country, but compelled, as it were, a recognition of woman's rights to dress as she pleases, and to fill any station, public or private, which capacity and inclination fit her for. In this sense she has been one of the greatest benefactors of her sex and of the human race."[10]

As was to be expected, the professional medical journals were more critical of Mary's performance than the general press. One declared that her opening remarks at St. James's were "as prosy as anything we had the ill fortune to hear in our student days." In its opinion she had harped on just one string, dress, and had spoiled a laudable desire for reasonable costume by her feminine vanity. It concluded that the lecture was an undertaking altogether above her powers, "and its only result has been to throw ridicule on herself, her sex, her profession, and her country, and to strengthen the opinions of those who hold that women had better not meddle in physic."

Another English medical review called her lecture "meagre and unsatisfactory to the utmost . . . vapid and thin with no intellectual grasp or solid foundation," and insisted that her "evident consciousness of sex was one of the characteristics which contributed to make the entertainment painfully ridiculous." Though written in a manner to suggest objectivity, the journal's reservations upon women practitioners are obvious. They might choose physic, but not with its recommendations, "and follow it through its wearisome and disgusting studies," but they were not justified in posing as orators in public houses.[11]

A third periodical styled her the "American Medical Nondescript."[12]

American medical reviews were ready to accept the interpretations of their English counterparts, and one journal published a lengthy letter from a former army surgeon, who had been a member of the medical board which had examined Mary at Chattanooga, excoriating her. He declared that the board found that she "had no more medical knowledge than an ordinary housewife, and that she was, of course, entirely unfit for the position of medical officer." He remembered, also, that she had claimed to have a medical diploma—"We did not see it"—from a "hydropathic institution at Geneva, New York. She had never been, so far as we could learn, within the walls of a medical college or hospital, for the purpose of obtaining a medical education."

The obvious inaccuracies in his statement were matched in his concluding paragraph in which he interpreted her capture. He alleged that her capture was designed by the War Department. "She was intended as a spy, and went forward to be captured. It was supposed that her sex and *profession* would procure her greater liberties and wider opportunities for observation than were at all possible to other prisoners. The medical staff of the army was made blind for the execution of this profound piece of strategy by the War Office—another instance of the esteem in which medical officers were held by the Hon. Secretary of War [Stanton]."[13]

Can it be that the surgeon's references to Mary's shortcomings as a physician were as fanciful as his spy story?

Mary accepted the hospitality of her new friends to travel and visit during December and through the holidays, and to complete the revisions of her lectures. She returned to the platform shortly after the advent of the new year.

On February 21 she again tackled an assignment at St. James's Hall, a benefit performance in behalf of the Bermondsey Poor Schools. She chose as her subject her captivity and imprisonment, and drew a "large and fashionable assembly." This time the occupants of the galleries came prepared to harass her from the start. She was greeted with a rash of "Whitechapel cat-calls," which ceased only when police intervened to remove the loudest among her tormentors, again reputed to be medical students. She then proceeded without further difficulties.[14] Several nights later she delivered an address on temperance at the Fetter Lane Chapel.

On March 6 she was in Hammersmith in West London speaking on her captivity and imprisonment, unquestionably her most popular subject. She was heard here with "deep and unbroken" attention interrupted only by "expressions of approval." Unfortunately, Mary was suffering from a distressing cough, and her remarks were interspersed with paroxysms, painful to both speaker and audience. But she refused to stop, and her coughing became less frequent. When she closed with a "gracful and eloquent tribute" to England and England's Queen, she was warmly applauded. She had discoursed for almost two hours.[15] The following night found her at Clapham Hall speaking on the same subject.

After a much-needed rest she was off to northern England for speaking engagements at New Castle, Blyth, Durham and Sunderland—all within a week. She was back in London for an address at the Peel Grove Institute in Hackney on March 30, and another at Camberwell, a London suburb, a few days later.

It is evident that the latter was strictly a commercial venture. The promoter there gave her directions, which would have destroyed any illusions to the contrary, to stay out of sight until curtain time, and then to go directly to the hall entrance, so that the public could not see her without paying the price of admission. "If you walk about there during day light, you can not expect people to pay for seeing you a second time. You must know that it is yourself that is the attraction and not the lecture."[16]

Her circuit next took her north and west of London, and included stops at Leicester, Manchester and Bristol. She then set out upon her most ambitious tour, arranged by a Glasgow entrepreneur, Monson Kyle, to the cities of Scotland. In just over a fortnight, beginning on April 26, she spoke in succession at Carlisle, Glasgow, Edinburgh, Kilmarnock, Dundee, Greenock, Ayr, Hamilton, and again in Glasgow. By the end of May she was back in the London periphery at Middlesex, Blackheath and Chelsea, with side trips to Chester and Brighton and elsewhere.[17] It was a giddy pace, and hardly compatible with her original quest for rest and relaxation. By April she was forced to reject invitations to lecture, rejections which must have been made reluctantly by the eager doctor.

Freed from the pressure of speech-making in June, Mary joined friends for a jaunt to Paris, a pleasure which she had contemplated for many years, and now given additional excitement by the Paris Exposition of 1867.

It had been opened officially a few weeks earlier by Emperor Napoleon III and the glamorous Empress Eugénie, and was for the moment the showplace of the world. Mary was present for the celebration attending the arrival of the Sultan of Turkey, and the awarding of the prizes. She heard the Emperor's address, and saw him halt unfinished when word was brought to him that his puppet Emperor in Mexico, Maximilian, had been executed by a firing squad.

A noted American journalist, Moncure Conway, also present, recalled that "We Americans found ourselves under the Mexican shadow." The French blamed American foreign policy for Maximilian's fate, and Exposition officials feared anti-American demonstrations. Two Fourth of July celebrations had been scheduled: one, to be held out of doors at the Exposition, was canceled; a dinner was permitted to go on as planned, when it was pointed out that it was a private American affair. However, some of the most distinguished visitors from the United States cautiously avoided it, while others who attended rejected invitations to speak. Many at the dinner refused to rise to toasts to President Andrew Johnson or to Emperor Napoleon III. The whole affair was proving to be flat and even boring.

But among the 300 participants was the irrepressible Dr. Mary, who had doubtless anticipated a gala commemoration. "Most of us were feeling the dinner dull," Conway reported, "when suddenly Dr. Mary Walker extemporized a sensation. Over her famous 'American Dress' she wore a large sash of stars and stripes. In this costume she walked up to the head of the table before the company, and before the amazed Milliken [James Milliken, of Philadelphia, presiding] could interfere, uttered a tribute to 'our soldiers and sailors,' dramatically kissed the flag she wore, and glided to her seat." Unfortunately, Conway did not relate the toastmaster's words, when he again found them. However, he did observe that "Dr. Mary did not wait for the dancing that followed and, when she left, received an ovation from the French crowd in the courtyard on account of the glorious independence of her trousers, nowise concealed but decorated by her patriotic sash. The applause must have been for Dr. Walker's independence; uglier dress was never worn."[18]

When not attending the Exposition Mary went sightseeing in Paris. In her perambulations she visited the Hôtel Dieu, one of

73

the great Parisian hospitals, where she was soon the toast of the interns.

The Paris correspondent of the *Lancet* (London) offered a colorful picture of her impact there:

A few days ago the even course of the medical service in the wards of the Hôtel-Dieu was agreeably broken by the unexpected visit of a female doctor—no less a personage than Miss Mary Walker, who is now well known in London. She had just come from the Santé, where she had been graciously received by M. Vulpeau, and now she was intent on going over the Hôtel-Dieu. The news soon spread through the wards, and shortly numbers gathered on her way to see what a confrere *en jupons* would look like. The peculiar costume of the lady added, of course, to the effect of the scene, and excited fresh curiosity. But the doctoress was in no way daunted, and walked composedly through the wards, rather pleased than otherwise. She wore on her breast the medal received from Congress, and it is said (the *bout de l'oreille* of female vanity would peep out) that she took some care to show it off to advantage. There was no medical conversation or inquiry, but towards the end of the visit the ice had been broken, and the interns of the Hôtel Dieu ventured to depute one of their number (a countryman of the doctoress) to invite her to breakfast with them in the *salle de garde*.

Their deputy, still ornamented with the classic white apron, gallantly offered his arm, and conducted his confrere to the *salle de garde*. There was a goodly gathering around the festive board, even a vice-professor of the Faculty had claimed the favour of a seat, and the greatest good humour and highest spirits enlivened the entertainment. The doctoress, who is a zealous teetotaler, would drink nothing but water; still there was drinking of healths, and a fraternal knocking of glasses, a quiet game of which concluded the proceedings of the memorable morning which will be noted henceforth as conspicuous in the annals of the *salle de garde* of the Hôtel-Dieu, and the doctoress left the hospital most satisfied with her warm reception; and impressed with the truth that the old reputation of the French for politeness and gallantry is still warranted, at least among the young medical portion of the community.[19]

Mary also made at least one visit to the Hospital of Charity. A French newspaper, commenting upon the incident, praised "Mme. Walker's" services in the Civil War as a doctor and surgeon. It found her petite and dignified, and observed that she was received with cordiality and respect by the doctors and students. Her presence there, it concluded, proclaimed a new principle in France, one which was already accepted in the New World, the equality of women in science.[20]

One additional comment upon Mary's impact upon Paris, a paragraph from an obscure English journal, bears repeating: "She has just returned from a four weeks' residence in Paris, where her costume attracted a large share of favorable notice. After being in public a few times she became so popular that she was constantly being invited to reunions of the best society. Her mission was brought under the notice of the Empress, who appears to take considerable interest in the reformed dress, as communications between her Imperial Majesty and Dr. Walker tend to show."[21]

The writer has found no other evidence of correspondence between Empress Eugénie and Mary. Mary once possessed a collection of autographs from distinguished persons, including President Lincoln, but presumably sold them when in need of funds. She was adept at name dropping, and it would appear that she would have found many occasions to mention the Empress' interest in dress reform. But there is only silence.

Back in England late in July, Mary spent her last fortnight in a frenzy of activities. She made no formal addresses, but presided at temperance and workingmen's conventions, and offered extemporaneous remarks before the Female Medical Society and the London Dialectical Society. Her most ambitious project was a gathering of women interested in dress reform in London on August 7. She called the meeting to discuss the advantages of the reformed dress, to exhibit its construction, and to form an association for its promotion throughout the country.[22] There was a good attendance, several ladies, in addition to Mary, appearing in the approved outfit. An organization was effected, with Mrs. Ellen Cooper of Sydenham, as president. The following morning Mary was in the cars for Liverpool and her return to the United States.

As the Liverpool packet churned the turbid North Atlantic, Mary had many hours to assess her experiences in retrospect. What had begun as a short visit for rest and recreation had become a vigorous lecture tour and crusade for dress reform stretching across a full year. She had demonstrated that she was news. She had attracted crowds in the streets as well as in the lecture halls. But was she simply an oddity, to be gaped at, as a theatrical promoter had reminded her, something to be seen, her message inconsequential? She could hardly have denied that such was the case for thousands of those who had flocked to see her. However, many had remained to listen. How could they hear of her experiences as a physician in the Union Army without acknowledging her services, and though her role was in many ways unique, without realizing that women, if permitted, might contribute immeasurably to human welfare and progress? How could they observe the practicality of her dress without feeling doubts about the artificialities of women's fashions, or how could the public see her in action and follow her through the press without reflecting upon the injustice of discriminations against women? Finally, how could English women fail to emulate her example? They had made a start. They had not only organized for dress reform but were actually wearing the costume. The revolution was gaining momentum!

Aside from long-range achievements Mary could take pride in her unprecedented success as a female lecturer in England. It had paid her expenses, and enabled her to lecture for philanthropic causes without charge. It is impossible to reconstruct her debits and credits, but she sometimes shared the profits with the management; on other occasions she was given the choice of sharing proceeds or receiving a guarantee of £10, plus transportation. Living expenses, meanwhile, aside from travel, were reduced by the generous hospitality of her friends. Her lecture on the war was the money-maker, and it would have lost interest with repetition. However, Mary did not press her luck, but concluded her appearances while they were still in demand.

She had arrived in England unheralded. By dint of her self-

76

confidence and poise, durability and adaptability, her flair for the dramatic, and of course, with a big assist from her bizarre costume, she had taken old England by storm—a truly notable achievement.

CHAPTER VII

LECTURER AND AUTHOR

Back in Washington after an exciting year in Europe, Mary discovered at once that she was no celebrity at home. Her triumphs abroad were with few exceptions ignored by the American press; nor were there organized interest groups, comparable to those in England, ready to provide her with audiences. But the stimulation of the lecture platform was in her blood, and she resolved to pick up here where she left off in Europe.

She projected a lecture tour through New England and New York with the story of her imprisonment in Castle Thunder as the principal attraction. Beginning in February of 1868 she spoke in Norwich and Willimantic, Connecticut, and in Utica, Schenectady and Amsterdam, New York. At Amsterdam her lecture was first scheduled in the Baptist Church, but opposition to her appearance in trousers forced its transfer to Union Hall. Mary seems to have had good receptions, but bookings were too sparse and distances too great to keep the venture solvent, and she concluded the tour after a three months' trial.[1]

She refused to admit defeat, however, and embarked upon a more extensive circuit the following year. Beginning at Cincinnati in September, 1869, she traveled westward through Missouri and Kansas, and thence south to Mississippi, Louisiana, and Texas. She seems to have started out with few bookings, depending upon newly formed groups for woman's rights, and picking up additional engagements when and where she could find them. Time was dimming the luster of her war experiences and the privations of a Confederate prison were scarcely suited to a speaking junket into the South. She appears to have been particularly interested in addressing Southern women, however, believing that her life in that region during the war had given her an intimacy with their needs and problems.

78

She met with a mixed response. In Fulton, Missouri, the local press acknowledged that "quite a respectable" audience assembled to see and hear the "somewhat celebrated not to say notorious" doctor. It conceded, also, that her enunciation and delivery were superior, but it wished that she would devote her talents to some "holier cause," and thereby "relieve her sex of the stigma she inflicts and the blush she engenders."[2]

At Kansas City, where she established headquarters for several weeks, her first appearance was spoiled by inclement weather. Only a small audience braved the driving snow to hear her deny that America was the land of freedom. No country, she maintained, was free where women could not vote. If women were equal to men socially, they should be equal also politically. She told of her attempt to vote after four years in the army. "But no, I was a woman and had to stand back." If a woman committed a crime, she was tried under man-made laws, by all-male juries—members of which were frequently not a woman's peers. She berated the males for perpetuating this system, and she was equally critical of women who refused to support the franchise because they believed it was inelegant and not in a lady's sphere of life. Such women, she insisted, had seen little of the world, and knew not what the poor working woman had to suffer.

Woman's suffrage would promote a better life. The moral courage of women, for example, would eliminate the sale of intoxicating beverages. Women could not leave such responsibilities to men; nor could wives expect better treatment from husbands unless they forced it from them. Men wanted to keep women bound together with whalebone, and tight-laced, but she would not accept their dictation. She had been arrested for her nonconformity, but would persevere. By 1899, she forecast, people would ridicule the critics of woman's rights, just as newspapers now censured its advocates. Mary repeated this theme, with minor variations, along her lecture trail.[3]

In Kansas City, only a few days after her reference to arrest for nonconformity in clothing, she was apprehended, by what proved to be an overzealous policeman, for her unbecoming clothing, and taken to a judge. Mary unleashed a torrent of abuse, first upon the policeman, and then upon the judge. The latter finally checked her, and speedily dismissed the case. The account of the incident in the local press ended with a parody in verse:

79

Policeman, spare those pants,
And don't make any row;
In youth, they sheltered me,
And I'll protect them now.[4]

Mary departed from Kansas City precipitously in search of an ephemeral pot of gold in Mississippi. She had received an appeal from a Mary L. Reed, of Port Gibson, to come to help organize a woman's society for the promotion of woman's rights. They needed her message and her counsel, and were prepared to pay $600 for an eminent lecturer, $450 of which had already been raised. They wished to schedule the meeting before the end of the year.

It was already mid-December when the invitation arrived. She replied that she would come at once, and would speak on December 28, or a few days later. She was so anxious to meet with leaders in Mississippi and other Southern states that she did not mind postponing several other engagements. "My heart is filled with *more* than *regard* for the Southern Sisterhood, for you like us must feel the degradation of all unfranchised women in a professed to be Republican Country."

She raced southward by rail and Mississippi steamer to reach her destination on time. Disillusionment followed. There was no Mary L. Reed and no woman's group; neither was there $600. The invitation had been a cruel hoax.[5]

It was a shattering experience, but Mary was made of stern stuff. She stopped at Vicksburg, where the scars of Grant's long siege seven years earlier were being covered. She spoke at the Opera House there, and in January delivered an address in the Assembly Hall of the State Capitol at Jackson. Incidentally, permission for her use of the hall was the first order of business of the newly reconstructed Carpetbag government of the state.

She was in New Orleans in February, just fifty-one years after her father's visit there, and was soon in the toils of the law. The police again found her costume obnoxious, and after the customary heated argument, spiced by Mary's sarcasms, she was released with the warning that she would be imprisoned if she appeared again in the offending clothing. Completely immune to such attempts to intimidate womankind, she ignored the admonition. Her pantaloons were on to stay!

80

She passed several months in the vicinity of New Orleans, delivering speeches in the neighboring parishes. In May she was in Texas. She lectured from several platforms in Austin, including the State Capitol, where she was introduced by Senator Petitt.

Here her tour ended. Her date book was empty, and her purse flat. But she had no regrets. Had she not presented her favorite issue to some thousands of hearers stretching across 3,000 miles? By June she was back in Washington after an absence of ten months.

Though her tour may have demonstrated that she could not live as a professional lecturer, it did not dampen her enthusiasm for exhortation. In October she delivered an address on temperance in New York, and in December spoke on woman's rights at Ottawa, the new Canadian capital. She also appeared frequently in the lecture halls of Washington. Speaking was always an exhilarating experience, and it never dulled from repetition. She was ever ready with a torrent of words.

Upon her return from her lecture tour Mary took time to complete a book which she had projected some years before. When finished it was a smallish, green-covered, 180-page volume bearing the enigmatic title *Hit*.[6] It was autobiographical, and brimmed over with her opinions upon a wide range of topics.

The frontispiece displayed a full-length engraving of the author, clad in the reformed dress: a knee-length tunic, with a small lacy Peter Pan collar, over long trousers. She dedicated it to: "My Parents, and also to the Practical Dress Reformers . . . and also to My Professional Sisters [Physicians] . . . and lastly to that Great Sisterhood, which embraces women with their thousand unwritten trials and sorrows that God has not given to men the power to comprehend. . . ."

In the preface she disclaimed any pretensions of saying everything upon marriage, or anything entirely original, but hoped that she might induce the reader to think calmly and profoundly upon it.

The text included chapters upon love and marriage, dress reform, tobacco, temperance, women's franchise, divorce, labor and religion. But whatever their titles, each documented man's inhumanity to woman, and forecast a bright new world wherein the former yielded to the latter her "God given rights." Despite her low opinion of the masculine sex, she appealed to their highest instincts to permit women to gain an equality, a goal which they could not realize otherwise, bound, as they were, by man-made laws.

"True conjugal companionship is the greatest blessing of which mortals can conceive in this life," she noted. Unfortunately, it was a rare phenomenon. To assume that marriages should endure through life, regardless of the consequences to the victims [usually female], because the marriage ceremony read, "What God has joined together," was utter hypocrisy. "He has had nothing to do with the matter, any more than suffering their consummation and continuance."[7] Courtship, which required that the female make no advances, but only wait, and ultimately accept rather than run the risk of spinsterhood, was man's making, not God's. A double moral standard for husband and wife, rigid divorce laws, varying from state to state, each contributing to woman's subjection in marriage, were man's responsibilities, not God's. She concluded her chapter with a resumé of marriage customs around the world.

Dress reform was essential for the health and well-being of the American woman, she insisted. Hair styles, for example, created unnatural pressures, and tight fitting clothing interfered with normal physical processes. Resulting physical malfunctions, in turn, contributed to mental and emotional disturbances. Hair should be free-flowing, and clothing should permit freedom of motion, and be arranged so as to require minimum vitality to carry it. While she did not require that women adopt men's attire, she set forth its advantages, and described in some detail an approved variation of it suited to women's needs. Man's role in making women victims of fashion was obvious. He set the ridiculous standards, cultivated the artificial in feminine tastes and styles, and required a slavish imitation of them. Meanwhile, man was careless of his own attire, insisting only that it be comfortable. "The greatest sorrows from which women suffer today," she averred, "are those physical, moral and mental ones, that are caused by their unhygienic manner of dressing! The want of the *ballot* is but a *toy* by comparison."[8]

Mary did not mean to imply, however, that the franchise was of secondary importance. It was a "Natural Right" denied by man, and the key to the "unqualified individuality" of woman. Political equality, she emphasized, would facilitate social equality. It would revolutionize marriage, since equals might live in harmony. The assumption that woman needed man's protection, and that she was incapable of exercising the full responsibilities of citizenship, was a man-made myth, and a subterfuge for man's tyranny. Irked by the argument that women should not govern since they could not defend their country in war, she delved into the past to find a host of heroines who had won renown on the battlefield. Addressing herself to her male readers, she added, "You are not our protectors. . . . If you were, who would there be to protect us from?"[9]

Tobacco and alcohol were evils because they were poisons. Assuming that the latter needed little documentation, she gave particular emphasis to the former. Tobacco ruined the digestive system, and its poisonous effects eventually reached every tissue. It produced paralysis and insanity, and left its blight upon the children of smokers, who were afflicted with digestive disorders and brain injury. Even the wife was not immune. She shrank from contacts with her tobacco-saturated husband, and suffered nervous exhaustion from the air which he contaminated. Mary also scored the vast sums spent for alcohol and tobacco, and the waste of soil, grains and fruit going into their production. But most of all she condemned their demoralizing effects upon marriage and women.

In her discussion of labor, Mary declared that all work was worthy, and deplored contemporary attitudes which held that some was degraded. She called for a greater recognition of the services of labor in making possible higher living standards, and cautioned employers against overburdening their employees. Overwork was harmful both to physical and mental health. Noting the significance of inventions in expanding production and reducing labor, she hailed the coming of an era when the working day would be reduced to three or four hours, and when the laborer would have leisure time to develop his mental powers.

Here again, she kept her focus upon women. Daughters as well as sons should be taught useful occupations, and they should receive equal pay for equal work. Low wages for men limited marriage opportunities, and the smaller pittances paid to females pushed them into ill-considered unions. She observed to the males that retirement from business, while a blessing, could not be an exclusive privilege. Yet, who had ever heard of a woman retiring? She urged men to take an interest in the household, and to share its responsibilities as an approach to a mutual retirement.

That these enlightened views on labor relations were not a fleeting impulse is suggested in an interview in New York more than twenty years later, in which she came to the defence of dancers at the Imperial Music Hall.

> The world at large, or society . . . doesn't think much of these actresses; but I lost most of my regard for society long ago. I think it is selfish and cruel. Now these poor girls who have to work so hard for a living have relatives. Even that poor girl whose acting consists altogether of kicking probably has a mother, and I have no doubt she is going through those gymnastic exercises to buy bread for the dear old soul. I am a woman, and I love women. That young woman is all right. There is that young lady who sings naughty songs. She does it for a livelihood. She's got a sweet face and she looks like a dear little woman. Bah! for the opinions of society.[10]

In her reflections upon religion Mary set forth the Golden Rule as an ideal. Where a father exemplified it, children learned to think of God as a father; where he was domineering they accepted God as a master. On the premise that religions were basically good, she urged a quiet toleration of diversity. By what name a particular denomination was known was not important. However, she insisted that none was true, "unless it is something that makes homes happy and ennobles life generally, by the precepts and examples of Christ, as embodied in the grandeur of the Golden Rule."[11]

Religious activity was equally significant for men and women. She denounced "misrepresentations" based on the writings of the Apostle Paul, which relegated women to a position of inferiority. Paul was writing for "slave-wives" of his own generation, she insisted. A so-called religion which reduced wives to servility was a hold-over from barbarism; religion was not designed to make women wretched. It is of interest to note that she was not altogether averse to dissensions in the home stemming from differences in religion, since it was sometimes the only issue upon

84

which a wife dared to take issue with her husband. Mary's out-
look was optimistic; religious groups adhering to the principles
of the Golden Rule would inevitably contribute "to make the marriage relations and homes generally, the dearest places and conditions on earth."[12]

Mary's religious practice was consistent with the basic philosophy expounded in *Hit*. Early in life she accepted Methodism, but
later severed her association, explaining, "Now I am a member
of every church in a sense. I have lived to see good in every
church, and to see good in every kind of an association, and to
affiliate with everything that is for the good and elevation of
humanity."[13]

Seven years after her initial venture as an author Mary published a second book with a longer but equally puzzling title:
Unmasked, or the Science of Immorality.[14] She covered much of
the same ground, but addressed herself to the masculine world
on the assumption that it was "natural to suppose men might
benefit by a treatise by a woman M.D." By "benefit" of course
she meant a more enlightened attitude toward woman's rights.

A notable feature of this second volume was its frank treatment of sex. A mere listing of the principal chapters indicates her
willingness to discuss subjects seldom found outside of medical
treatises—subjects, in fact, which would be discreetly covered in
a plain wrapper in the sophisticated mid-twentieth century: hermaphrodites, morning sickness, kissing, hymens, seminal weakness, barrenness, social disease.

In her introductory chapter she deplored the manner in which
men learned about sex, that is, by word of mouth, older boys
repeating to their younger playmates "the most degraded ideas
of life, and only such parts as are demoralizing and filled with
the grossest errors." They talked over the arts of seduction, and
grew to manhood thinking it clever to take advantage of women.
Fed upon such distortions, the typical male lacked high moral
standards, and when confronted with his infidelities offered the
stock answers that he was as good as any other man. Men assumed it was proper to have sexual relations with women outside
of marriage because they were men. She conceded, however, that
all males were not alike, and catalogued them rather neatly according to the degree to which they strayed from the "straight
and narrow":

Code I—Man who truly respected his wife, and treated
    her with the same deference as his honored mother
    or sister. (This type was quite uncommon.)
Code II—Man who first "sowed his wild oats," and then
    married a pure girl and assumed there was none better
    than he.
Code III—Similar to Code II, but man continued to have
    sexual relations with so-called respectable women.
Code IV—Man who had women in various places simul-
    taneously, and deserted them as he tired of them.
Code V—Man who visited houses of prostitution for
    extra-marital relations.
Code VI—Man who was constantly on the prowl for vic-
    tims to satiate his sexual drives.[15]

She maintained that the happiest marriage was one in which
there was equality between husband and wife. A husband who
had sexual relations with the "vile," whether before or during
marriage, inevitably injured his nervous system, and transmitted
the effects of his unchastity to his children, who were born sickly
and susceptible to disease. She traced many deformities among
infants to sexual excesses and abuses.

In her chapter on hermaphrodites she went into detail to
describe a variety of deformities, some of which she declared that
she had seen, though most were based on hearsay. She attributed
to men a condition not unlike morning sickness among women
when in pregnancy, and explained that it was brought on by the
husband's emotional reaction to the condition of his wife. She
went so far as to report cases among husbands when they were
removed many miles from their wives. Though the germ theory
of disease was still several decades away, she found kissing a bad
practice, and injurious to children, especially if kissed on the
mouth. Syphilis, she maintained, had been transmitted by kissing.

She argued that men, while giving little heed to their own
chastity, overemphasized the hymen as proof of virginity among
women. She cited evidence of conception in which the hymen
remained intact; and conversely, situations in which the hymen
was broken without sexual intercourse.

Seminal weakness, she advised, was a natural and monthly
tendency, and did not suggest depravity. Barrenness was fre-

quently caused by sexual excesses, but she acknowledged that there were physical factors involved also. She interpreted the social evil to include the effects of tobacco and alcohol upon marriage, and also the deleterious effects of women's fashions.

It was a book which required courage to write, and though certainly not so intended by the author, affords the reader an insight into the folklore and old wives' tales which still passed for science in 1878. More significant than its contributions to medical and social science, however, was its obvious appeal for women's rights.

There appears to be no information on the book's sale, but it seems unlikely that it turned up on many book shelves, despite the good intentions of the writer.

CHAPTER VIII

SUFFRAGETTE

During the years immediately following her return from England, when not on the lecture platform, Mary devoted most of her time and energy to the crusade for woman's rights. It was a strenuous but rewarding life, encompassing the broad range of activities of the professional lobbyist. She made her headquarters in Washington, boarding and rooming with a small band of fellow professionals. A small house shared with Mrs. Belva Lockwood was for a time a woman's rights cell, where a core of dedicated disciples planned their strategy.

When Congress was in session they focused upon the various committees responsible for matters affecting women: judiciary, pensions, and territories, including the District of Columbia. They also prepared articles for the press, and published a variety of pamphlet materials. When Congress adjourned, and Washington momentarily lost its significance, the reformers were off to a round of conventions and speaking engagements, and in Mary's case to resume her frequently neglected medical practice. Unlike some of her associates, she had not inherited wealth to draw upon or a husband to pick up her checks.

At this time Mary was at the crest of the woman's rights movement, appearing on the same platforms with Lucy Stone, Susan B. Anthony, Mary Livermore, Belva Lockwood and the others. She frequently received more than her share of attention in the press, presumably because she was newsworthy, and her appearances colorful and controversial.

Mary's activities in Washington first broke into print in May, 1868, when she addressed the Universal Franchise Association upon her experiences and impressions of the progress of woman's suffrage agitation in Europe. At the conclusion of this meeting a substantial delegation of suffragists appeared before the Judiciary Committee of the House of Delegates, which at that time was the legislative body of the District of Columbia, in support of a bill giving women the right to vote in the District.

Mary and Belva Lockwood were the spokesmen for the delegation. The latter, who had been a teacher in western New York prior to her marriage to Dr. Ezekiel Lockwood, was particularly effective. She reminded the committee that its chairman, G. H. Burgess, had once been a student of hers, yet she was ineligible to vote. The absurdity of the situation was not lost upon the committee. They expressed their sympathies for the wishes of the suffragists, but insisted that they had no discretion in the matter since the organic law specified "male" suffrage. To demonstrate that there was no doubt regarding the intentions of Congress, they called attention to the fact that a motion by George W. Julian to strike out the word "male" had been defeated by a large majority in the House of Representatives.[1]

The following year the dress reformers, a group which Mary had helped to organize just before the war, and which she had headed for several years, held a convention in the national capital. They had broadened their goals, and were now identified as the Mutual Dress Reform and Equal Rights Association. Mary opened the proceedings, conducted before a large audience in Union League Hall, with a short speech upon the merits of dress reform. She was followed by her old friend, Dr. Lydia Hasbrouck, who elaborated upon the unhealthfulness of current fashions, and scored the critics of the reformed dress. As an illustration, she referred to newspaper accounts of the alleged refusal of President Grant to receive their associate, Dr. Walker, unless she were dressed in the usual feminine clothes.

Dr. Hasbrouck's remarks stirred Mary to further oratory. She declared that General Grant had not refused to see her in her reformed costume; in fact she had not called at the White House since his inaugural a few months before. However, she had no fears that she would be refused admittance. She had attended Mrs. Grant's receptions, she declared, and had been treated courteously.

Incidentally, Mary saved an invitation to Grant's inaugural ball, and filed it with her personal papers.

Reverting to an observation by Dr. Hasbrouck that the dress reform movement was viewed with suspicion by many women, Mary consoled her audience with the assurance that no great reformers had ever escaped calumny and persecution. Every advantage which had been won, she insisted, had been gained "through the sorrows of some reformer; the first user of an umbrella was denounced as too effeminate; Columbus had his persecutors, and others advancing new ideas met with nothing but scorn from the masses." She resumed her seat amid warm applause.[2]

Despite Mary's call for courage in the face of ridicule, the rejection of the reformed dress by the vast majority of women was disheartening to its advocates. To bear such epithets as "cranks," "idiotic eccentricities," "fearfully hybrid," "anomalous creatures," and "thirsting for vulgar notoriety," from women as well as men, required a rare brand of fortitude. And if this were not sufficient to discourage the dress reformers from venturing beyond the confines of their homes, children added to their torment, making them targets of ridicule as they followed them in the streets. To hear: "Doctor, give me a chew of tobacco," or "Pull down your vest," or possibly, "There goes Doctor Mary and her Dad," from a gang of boys, took almost as much courage as to endure the somewhat more sophisticated barbs of their elders.

It turned out that few were prepared to fight the battle, year after year, and decade after decade, and most of the small band of reformers eventually packed away their pantaloons in chests, and wore them no more. And very few of this generation lived as long as Mary to see the sudden revolution in women's clothing which accompanied World War I. Perhaps if they had found a Marlene Dietrich in 1869 things might have gone differently, but even Marlene might have been crushed by the Victorian sense of propriety. It is interesting to note that one columnist, who sensed the need for glamor in the movement, advised that it might win out if Empress Eugénie could be enlisted to don the controversial costume.

But with Mary, attack simply called forth a counter-offensive. Instead of discarding pants, she made her attire increasingly mannish. By the 1880s there was scarcely a feminine touch: a man's coat and pants, shirt, stiff collar and tie, and even a tall silk hat. Only a cape, sometimes worn over her coat, hinted that there was a woman behind the masculine facade.

But this was some years in the future. There was still much that was feminine, and even dainty in her appearance during these postwar years in Washington.

In June, 1869, Mary lectured at the Union League Hall in Washington on the subject, "Pure Love and Sacred Marriage." Introduced by Belva Lockwood, she was heard by what was described as a good-sized audience.

In August she was in Philadelphia participating in the National Working Men's Convention. Her official authorization as a member was a note signed by Belva Lockwood which certified that "Dr. Mary E. Walker is connected with the Woman's Labor Movement in this city [Washington], and is an accredited delegate for the Working Women of Washington."[3]

A month later Mary went with other leaders of woman's rights to Cincinnati to help found the Women's Suffrage Association for Ohio. Much of the discussion there was directed toward the adoption of resolutions, of which the proposition that, "Women as a class, have special interests as wives, mothers and widows, and that these interests should be directly represented in the government," drew the most vigorous defence. Susan B. Anthony and Lucy Stone led off with impassioned critiques of a society in which men arrogated to themselves the power over women and children. At the close of the latter's remarks a reporter noted that, "Dr. Mary Walker rose from her seat at the back of the stage, and came slowly forward. Immediately all eyes were turned on the slight, strangely attired form, and the lean and hungry countenance. . . . She stood still for a moment, quiet and self-possessed under the gaze of a thousand people, and the closest observer might have looked in vain for the flush that never comes to her pale face."

She had risen, she said, to support the arguments of her predecessors, giving emphasis to the injustice of discriminatory, man-made laws. She had only scorn for men who justified legal codes on the assumption that they were designed to protect women, and she was equally scornful of women who saw no need for laws which would make them the equal of their brothers. But she predicted that the time was coming when they must see its necessity. "How well we remember the time when the Negroes were downtrodden," she continued, "when they had no human or political rights; but just as soon as the ballot was placed in their hands, they not only had all that the ballot could give them, but those rights were secured to them which were away beyond the sphere of legislation." [This, of course, was the Carpetbag era, and be-

91

fore resurgent white supremacy again made the Negro a political cipher.] "So with you, the wives, the mothers and the daughters of the men of this intelligent State of Ohio, so will it be with you when you can walk up to the polls and stand side by side with your husbands, fathers, brothers and sons. . . . I hope this resolution will pass. I know that in the hearts of thousands of women that have not spoken, there is a feeling of anxious and earnest interest in regard to this matter, and they are looking to those who dare to speak and contend for the enfranchisement of women."[4]

When she sat down the resolution was adopted by a unanimous vote. Having completed its deliberations upon the resolutions, the convention drafted a constitution and by-laws, and elected officers for the permanent organization of the Ohio association.

With the business completed Miss Anthony delivered what was scheduled as the final address, but as she finished there were calls from the audience for Dr. Walker. They elicited a quick response. "The unique little lady in slabsided silks and elongated curls, tripped mincingly forward, and passing one pantalooned continuation behind the other, fetched a prim bow in acknowledgment of a perfect outburst of cheers and catcalls." The accolade might have stopped here without a word from Mary. But Mrs. Mary Livermore, one of the veterans of the suffrage movement, a tireless worker in the Civil War, and a Brahmin with a highly developed sense of propriety, jumped from her chair on the platform and asked to be heard. She was recognized, and proceeded to scold the audience for their improper conduct. Ladies and gentlemen, she emphasized, did not indulge in catcalls and hootings.

The situation was difficult, and might have been disastrous, but Mary handled it admirably. She declared that she did not feel that anything disrespectful was intended. At the front during the war Ohio men [There was an obvious masculine undertone in the shouting.] and Ohio regiments were always glad to hear her name and to show her respect. She knew that when they heard of her imprisonment by the Rebels, they dropped their cards at play and shed tears. She knew, too, that there was something good about man—beneath his exterior there always throbbed a noble and generous nature. [This from Mary!] She stopped, to a prolonged applause.

When it ceased she addressed the throng on woman's rights. Unfortunately, her words were not recorded. But it is of interest to note that the Cincinnati papers gave her more attention than any of the other professionals at the convention.[5]

Mary left Cincinnati for a speaking tour which continued well into the following year. But in 1871 she was back in Washington, fighting the battle for woman's rights. In February she delivered at the National Theater a lecture which she titled "National Salvation." She developed her topic historically, dwelling minutely upon the causes of the Civil War and the characteristics of the corrupt rings which beset the nation at this time. Most of the scandals of the Grant era had not yet come to light, but the Tweed Ring in New York and the Whiskey Ring had produced headlines. She hailed the work of women in temperance reform, and declared that they might render similar contributions in behalf of governmental reforms. She then launched upon the injurious effects of corsets and long skirts. Only through their elimination would women have the vitality to pursue their true mission. She closed with a plea for legislation to guarantee that "the right of women as citizens of the United States to vote shall not be denied or abridged by any State or Territory on account of sex." Only when this goal was realized would the nation have true republicanism.

The lecture was well attended, and Mary repeated it two weeks later at the same hall.[6]

It is of interest to note that Mary became increasingly hostile toward President Grant, despite her identification with the war. Possibly it was his failure to endorse woman's suffrage, or more likely, his indifference toward temperance reform. In any event, by 1870 Mary was openly critical of his consumption of strong drink. In an address to the Sons of Temperance she cited instances in which Grant became so befuddled with intoxicating drinks that he had to be taken home by his friends. Love of liquor, she held, had made him torpid, leaving his intellectual capacities inferior to those of his Secretary of State, Hamilton Fish.[7]

At this time, also, Mary served as a member of the Central Women's Suffrage Bureau, organized in Washington to coordinate activities relating to suffrage. They sponsored a law class for women in the Free National University, which later granted a law degree to Belva Lockwood. They solicited funds to endow a chair of medicine at Howard University to be filled by a woman professor, gave their official support to the work of Victoria Woodhull, an extremely controversial English feminist, and supported woman's suffrage in the states and territories. Of particular interest was a pending bill for the government of the District of Columbia, which the suffragists hoped to amend so as to give residents a share of self-government, including the ballot for women. At a mass meeting in March a committee was named to wait on Congress, and urge the amendment of the bill. With the business completed, shouts for Doctor Walker brought Mary to the platform. To an audience composed largely of men, she declared that they were now tasting what women of America had experienced all of their lives, that is, disfranchisement. It only proved that women were needed in Congress to prevent the passage of ill-considered legislation.[8]

Failing to make headway in their bid for home rule and woman's suffrage in Washington, suffragists decided upon a more direct approach to secure the vote. They drew up petitions requesting that their names be registered as qualified voters in the districts in Washington in which they lived. They then presented the petitions in person and requested that election officials register them. Mary was in the vanguard of this maneuver. Early on election day she sent a note to the election board stating that a large number of women would present themselves for registration that afternoon. "Mrs. Lockwood, Dr. Mary E. Walker and others came in the first carriage and passed through the crowd with respectful attention having been shown them by the mixture of masculine voters that were waiting all around. Carriage after carriage, under the direction of the just-mentioned ladies, continued to arrive, and finally a large number of women on foot made their appearance."[9] When all had arrived they marched into the marshal's office. At the head of the procession was Mrs. Lockwood, followed by her husband, Dr. Ezekiel Lockwood. Then, in order of succession, came Mary, Mrs. Sara J. Spencer, Mrs. Sarah P. Edson, Dr. Susan Edson, Dr. Caroline Winslow and Mrs. Josephine S. Griffin. Each carried a bouquet for the member who would register her. Frederick Douglass, the famed

Mary Walker, Age Twelve
Mary, at right, with her sister, Aurora Borealis

Dr. Mary Walker
This painting of Dr. Walker hangs in the Medical Museum of the
Armed Forces Institute of Pathology, Washington, D.C.

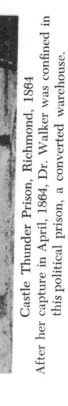

Dr. Walker in 1865
This photograph of the doctor is
in the National Archives

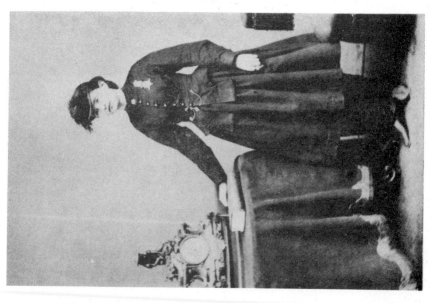

Castle Thunder Prison, Richmond, 1864
After her capture in April, 1864, Dr. Walker was confined in
this political prison, a converted warehouse.

Dr. Walker's Decorations
The Congressional Medal of Honor is
at the left of the photograph.

Dr. Walker in England, 1867
An engraving from a photograph by Messrs. Elliot & Fry

A Visiting Celebrity
Photograph of Dr. Walker on the front page
of a London paper, 1867

Dr. Mary E. Walker, Suffragette
This photograph was taken in 1880, when Dr. Walker was
pioneering in the fight for woman's rights, especially suffrage.

Immodesty?

On the occasion of Dr. Walker's arrest in New York in 1871, the press commented on the absurdity of the charge of immodesty.

Dr. Walker Wearing Her Fur Cape
This photograph was taken in Oswego, N. Y., around 1905

A Concession to Femininity?
In this 1908 photograph, Dr. Walker wears a rose in her vest.

Three Pioneers of Woman's Rights
Dr. Walker with Reverend Susana Harris and Attorney Belva
Lockwood, who ran for President in 1884 and 1888, in Oswego,
around 1908.

Going to Her Office
This photograph, taken in Oswego around 1916, suggests the
complete acceptance of Dr. Walker by her fellow townsmen.

Negro orator, joined the line of march at this point. They stopped in front of the registration desk, presented their petition to the chairman, and asked to be registered. The officials managed the affair with dignity, but it was obvious that tempers were short.

General Crocker mounted a bench and replied for the registrars that they were unanimously of the opinion that under the law none but males could register. Whatever their personal feelings might be, they could not violate the law. They would not register them.

At this point Mary, as spokesman for the pressing throng, stepped forward. The tumult ceased. "Gentlemen," she said, "these women have assembled to exercise the right of citizens of a professed-to-be republican country, and if you debar them of the right to register, you but add new proof that this is a tyrannical government, sustained by force and not by justice. As long as you tax women and deprive them of the right of franchise, you but make yourselves tyrants. You imprison women for crimes you have forbidden women to legislate upon."

She was interrupted, and given a slip of paper written, it was reported, by a registrar who preferred to remain anonymous. She quickly scanned it, then read: "The law does not say that women *shan't* vote." Encouraged to find a hint of support, she continued to belabor the male sex as the so-called protectors of women. When a member of the board intervened to say, "You must marry a voter to get a protector," her invective became more biting. She declared that they had not come there to marry voters, and there would be enough time to think of marriage when vile tobacco and whiskey were no longer used by man. If they really had as much moral courage as women, they would register them, and abide the consequences.

She failed to move the registrars from their determination to uphold the law and convention, but she was warmly applauded by the assemblage. She also received at least one favorable notice in the press. "Many of her hearers . . . had never listened to any *argument* before on this question . . . and after the women had departed the various points were discussed, and those men heretofore bitterly opposed were heard to say that they would not hereafter throw any barriers in the way of women voting. All the array of women that appeared to register would have had but little effect toward converting the crowd to the propriety of such a course had it not been for this speech." The Washington strategy to gain the ballot was to be repeated in many communities the following year.[10]

A month after her tilt with the election board Mary and other feminists, including Mrs. Isabella Beecher Hooker, Mrs. Paulina Wright Davis and Susan B. Anthony, addressed the National Woman's Suffrage Convention in Washington. A few weeks later she was in New York participating in another meeting of this organization. She congratulated the suffragists for their attempt to register in Washington; they had done more for the vote, she declared, than all the conventions ever held. She urged the passage of a declaratory law by Congress as the simplest means of giving the ballot to women, emphasizing that it would save almost endless labors in the various states.[11]

Meanwhile, Mary and Belva Lockwood collaborated to sustain the momentum of the woman's movement in the capital. In the summer of 1871 Mary spent some weeks in New York, reporting on women's activities there for the *Washington Gazette*, while Belva held the fort on the banks of the Potomac. "Our house has been a continuous resort for all of the woman's rights folks ever since you left," Belva advised Mary. Her report on the latter's articles was not encouraging, however. They had not been published, and she had found the editor evasive about future acceptances.[12]

Mary's future was not as a columnist, and she seems to have discontinued it after a short trial, and returned to Washington.

The following winter suffragists collected petitions from all corners of the nation requesting Congress to pass a declaratory law, which would make women as well as Negroes beneficiaries of the Fifteenth Amendment. The petitions were pieced together to create one of mammoth proportions, 240 feet long, with some 35,000 signatures. With this petition in hand, Belva and Mary and a host of followers descended upon the Capitol, intending to deliver it to Benjamin Butler, the controversial Civil War General, who had insulted Southern womanhood or at least jarred Southern chivalry by his infamous Order Number 28 at New Orleans. He was now a Representative from Massachusetts. For a time he could not be located, and Belva and Mary scurried about the corridors in quest of him. It was a race against time; but they won. Butler found an empty committee room, seated himself behind a desk, and invited the women to present their case.

But here things went wrong. Mrs. Isabella Beecher Hooker obtained the floor and charged that Mrs. Lockwood had initiated the action without proper authorization, and that the Woman Suffrage Association would not be responsible for it. Her claim was denied by Mary, who informed the bewildered Butler that "whether it was to be a feast or a funeral, it was Mrs. Lockwood's," and that Mrs. Hooker had nothing to do with it. Sensing that Mrs. Lockwood was in command, the former general called upon her, and she presented the petition. He graciously accepted it and urged that even larger petitions be forthcoming. The ladies then withdrew, and crowded into the galleries of the House of Representatives, where the sometimes gallant Ben. Butler presented the petition. It was referred to the Judiciary Committee, where of course it was buried.[13]

At the annual Woman Suffrage Association convention in 1872 the declaratory act and mass registration approaches to woman suffrage were given official endorsement. Both, of course, had been ardently championed by Mary and Belva Lockwood for several years. Several hundred women went home from the convention to demand that they be registered. Among them was Mary, who later described her experience as follows:

> When I walked up to the ballot box [in Oswego Town], one of the election officers ordered me out of the place. Instead of going, I gave him a piece of my mind, and insisted that I had a right to vote. Then another officer hunted up a law which stated that nobody but a male citizen, twenty-one years of age, should be allowed to vote.
>
> "Are you a male citizen," he asked in a ferocious manner. "No, sir," I answered. "Well, then you can't vote." And I didn't either.[14]

Most of the other suffragettes experienced similar refusals, and some took their cases to court.

One, which took a slightly different twist, occurred in Rochester, New York, where Susan B. Anthony cast ballots in the state and congressional elections. She was indicted for voting illegally, and fined, though the fine was never paid. Three cases stemming from these attempts to register and vote reached the United States Supreme Court. In each test the privilege was denied.

This defeat was a turning point in Mary's leadership in the crusade for woman's rights. Heretofore, though her unorthodox costume and her aggressiveness sometimes alienated conservative leaders, she was in the main current of the movement, and sharing platforms with Lucy Stone and Susan B. Anthony.

But the failure to obtain the ballot through mass registrations and the declaratory act convinced most of the suffragists that success hinged upon an amendment to the Constitution: a Sixteenth Amendment, which would guarantee the vote for women as the Fifteenth had done for the Negro. Having plotted this course, they pursued it relentlessly until 1919, when the Nineteenth—not the Sixteenth—Amendment brought their bark into port.

But not Mary. She had accepted what, in her judgment, was a simple, direct and practical approach, and she would not deviate to follow the party line. She was soon relegated to the radical fringe of the movement, and was never readmitted to the councils of the association.

Her decision to go it alone also terminated her association with Belva Lockwood, heretofore her best friend and most ardent supporter among the feminists. A daughter of Belva, in an unpublished biography of her mother, commented upon the relationship of Mary and Belva:

"Attending President Arthur's New Year's reception together one year," she recalled, "the two women made a sharp contrast; Belva, tall and stately, was attired in a handsome, blue velvet and distinctly feminine gown. Doctor Walker, small with short hair and pinched features, wore black trousers and frock coat in one hand carrying a man's silk hat, in the other a thin walking stick." But Belva eventually concluded that Mary's bizarre costume and the hostility which it engendered retarded the woman's rights crusade. "On one occasion she attempted to remonstrate with her about it. Doctor Mary flew into such a rage that the subject was never again mentioned."[15]

Certainly by 1874, if a statement by a second daughter of Belva reflected the latter's attitude, the friendship had cooled. Writing a column from Washington for a newspaper in Lockport, New York, she observed:

There stalks about our city unmolested by the police a curious compound of flesh and blood which has the appearance of being "neither man nor beast, but altogether ghoul." It is clad in pants cut like a man's, and a half-fitting basquine with a skirt reaching to the knee; a head of short curls is surmounted by a woman's hat. The wearer of the promiscuous dress is called Dr. Mary Walker.

She was born in Oswego, N. Y. She is supposed to have studied medicine and to be entitled to M.D. She has been married and divorced but declines to be called Mrs. She was in the army and has presented a small bill of $10,000 for services which Congress has thus far declined to settle. She was offered a place as clerk in the Treasury if she would accept a woman's dress but although impecunious she refused to sacrifice her principle for $75 or $80 per month. She delights to attend public assemblies and if permitted will always make a speech. She sits with limbs crossed but eschews man's favorite vice, tobacco. She claims to be a *suffering* woman, but takes no stock in Miss Anthony. She may have her mission but people have failed to see fruits of her good work.[16]

Mary's break with the leadership did not deter her from waging her own crusade. Though an outsider now, she turned up at convention after convention for more than forty years. At the 1877 convention of the Woman Suffrage Association she appeared with a petition containing her views on suffrage, and circulated it among the members. Calls for her to speak became so numerous that they interrupted the proceedings, but the leaders refused to recognize her. According to Mary's version of the incident, the din continued until she stood at her seat and requested silence.[17]

A few weeks after this convention, however, Mary's prestige in the association was still recognized sufficiently to permit her to serve on a committee of three, with Mary A. Tillotson of New Jersey, and Mrs. N. Cromwell of Arkansas, to testify before the Judiciary Committee of the House of Representatives in support of woman suffrage.

A short time later, also, she and Sara Andrews Spencer addressed a House subcommittee on Territories in opposition to a measure proposing the disfranchisement of women in Utah Territory as a means of suppressing polygamy there. Utah, incidentally, though infamous in the minds of suffragettes for its polygamy, was one of the several Territories at this time to legalize woman suffrage, and was thus for the feminists a model for the benighted states of the East.[18]

But Mary's status with the leadership continued to deteriorate. She is responsible for the story that at the convention of the association in 1898, the managers called off a scheduled final session after her supporters had forced them to put her on the program, preferring to "disgrace one woman," rather than make "simpletons of those who had been laboring for years for a constitutional amendment."[19]

On other occasions Mary was so obnoxious to the more conservative inner core that they refused to permit her to pay a nominal registration fee, so that they could deny her the privilege of being heard.[20]

Between conventions she prepared handbills, dispatched memorials to Congress, and addressed audiences at fairs, Grange halls, farmers' picnics, Memorial Day celebrations, and others. She was still pleading her case in 1907, when she published a pamphlet titled:

Crowning Constitutional Argument
of
MARY E. WALKER, M.D.
OSWEGO, N. Y.
1907
Woman's Franchise . . . Final Argument

The document is of interest in that it is one of the most comprehensive statements of Mary's approach to woman's suffrage. She cited cases in New Jersey and Maryland to indicate that women who met local property qualifications had sometimes voted in colonial days; and women in the other colonies, she argued, did not lose their right to vote because they had not used it.

The Federal Constitution was written in behalf of "We the

100

People," which included women. It was designed to create a republic, and in Article IV, Section 4, guaranteed to every state in the union a republican form of government. For the states to deny the vote to women was to reduce the nation to half-republican. The situation might be speedily corrected if the states simply passed statutes declaring null and void all disabilities heretofore adopted against women. And since Article I, Section 2, of the Federal Constitution gave the franchise in Congressional elections to electors in the states qualified to vote for state assemblymen, women would automatically qualify also to vote for members of the House of Representatives.

She claimed that she had presented her case to Senator Charles Sumner and Chief Justice Chase as early as 1871. Both were sympathetic, and the former had assured her that "her argument was *true*, and that no jurist had seen the Constitution of the United States in its true light regarding women; and a woman's brain had seen it; and it opened the door through which all women would walk and vote."

The tract next detailed her efforts to spread her "Crowning Constitutional Argument," and the opposition which she had faced from "Sue" Anthony, Dr. Anna Shaw, and other leaders of the Woman Suffrage Association. They had resorted to a variety of tricks to silence her and to thwart the distribution of the pamphlet. But she had not been diverted.

Mary made the dissemination of the "Crowning Constitutional Argument" one of her major activities, and saw to it that Presidents, legislators and governors were well supplied.

In 1911 she had the satisfaction of seeing her panacea for woman's legal inferiority introduced in the legislature by Oswego County's Assemblyman, Thaddeus C. Sweet. It declared that any law which discriminated against women, and denied them the privileges accorded to men should be deemed in conflict with the United States Constitution, and should be construed to confer equal privileges.

When the bill came before the Judiciary Committee for consideration, Mary appeared, and delivered an extended address in its support. She also answered numerous questions and advised the members to reread the Constitution of the United States that they might be convinced that it implied equality for women. Despite her impassioned plea, the bill died in committee.[21]

101

Even as the Nineteenth Amendment snow-balled toward victory, she persisted in her point of view. Her appearances before committees of Congress and the New York Legislature were now identified as hostile, in opposition to the Amendment.

In 1912 before the Judiciary Committee of the House of Representatives, she refused to acknowledge the propriety of Congressional action on the suffrage amendment. They might just as well "grant women the right to wear gum shoes." Women, she averred, had always had the right to vote; and she repeated her "Crowning Constitutional Argument" to prove it. When she had first advocated its approach in 1871, it had been too novel for immediate acceptance. But the time was now ripe. She deplored the time wasted by busy legislators in listening to the endless delegations of the Woman Suffrage Association. And when the Chairman dissented, declaring that the association's appearance could not be termed a waste of time, she retorted, "That is chivalry." Mary's remarks filled fourteen pages of the Committee's report.[22]

Two years later she was again before the Judiciary Committee with the same arguments; and in 1916, when eighty-three, she was back once more, refusing to bow to the inevitable acceptance of the Nineteenth Amendment. To her usual plea she added an indictment of the "Anna Shaw Clique" for denying her the platform and interfering with the distribution of the "Crowning Constitutional Argument" at their recent national convention in Washington. This, despite the fact that she was the oldest suffragette in the assemblage. She insisted that their strategy had not been completely successful, however. At the College Women's Association banquet at the close of the sessions, she had presented "enough of the 'Argument' in a clear voice to make the Southern delegation and many of the Middle Western states and the Eastern states thoroughly disgusted with the action of the Shaw woman," and had supplied them with 150 copies of her tract.[23]

The New York State Constitutional Convention of 1915 for a time diverted Mary's focus to Albany. Determined to block woman suffrage in the state through the amending process, she appealed to the Chairman of the Suffrage Committee, Patrick W. Cullinan, a resident of Oswego, for an opportunity to address the convention. When it did not immediately materialize, she asked

Luther Mott, Oswego's Congressman, to intervene with a request to Elihu Root, the chairman of the convention. Mary went so far as to offer a sample letter, which he might forward to Root. "For while she is a Democrat," it read in part, "we can not afford to deny a request that she claims as a United States Constitutional right."[24] She also reminded Mott that President Wilson would have been willing to appoint her as Postmaster of Oswego, if he had been able to overcome the Postmaster General's preference for the incumbent. Mott seems not to have consulted Root, but instead forwarded Mary's request with her sample letter, and an accompanying note to Cullinan. In the latter he referred to Mary as a "distinguished constituent." Cullinan, meanwhile, advised Mary that he had introduced a resolution, requesting that she be permitted to address the convention, and that it had been referred to the Committee on Rules.[25]

Mary eventually settled for an opportunity to testify before the Suffrage Committee, though with some misgivings since her relations with Judge Merrick Stowell, a second Oswego member on the Committee, were strained.

Appearing as a hostile witness, she repeated her "Crowning Constitutional Argument," and insisted that the legislature pass an act nullifying all laws and court decisions which discriminated against women, and not meddle with the Constitution. "I am opposed to granting men the right to vote on the *rights* of women. It is an unconstitutional usurpation of power." They had no more authority to pass on the franchise for women than did carpenters to decide upon the voting rights of farmers. Thus she placed herself squarely against the bill to amend the state constitution which had twice passed the legislature, and would soon go before the electorate for a referendum.

She described her efforts in behalf of woman suffrage in England in 1866, observing that she had advised women to go to the polls, justifying it as property holders and taxpayers under English laws. Some 10,000, she insisted, had done so in 1867. She deplored the "hoodlum class" in England, who were agitating for the ballot by smashing windows, destroying the Kew Gardens and putting acids into mail boxes, and branded the hunger strikers as "demented."[26]

She also had some caustic remarks for Dr. Anna Shaw, the distinguished President of the National American Woman Suf-

103

frage Association, charging her with interference, when she had attempted to speak before the Judiciary Committee of the New York Assembly four years before. Incidentally, excerpts from Mary's testimony were included in New York's Freedom Train in 1949. It was not made clear in this exhibit, however, that on this occasion Mary was actually blocking a plan for suffrage.

Mary was enthusiastic over her performance, and urged Cullinan to have her remarks published and distributed without delay. She also advised him to assume the leadership in support of her plan for woman's suffrage, and predicted that it would make him the next Governor. Women would be grateful to him, regardless of their party affiliations. She promised him her vote as a "high class Democrat," despite his Republicanism. "Now strike while the iron is hot! It is the opportunity of your life." But Cullinan did not strike, and he was never Governor![27]

CHAPTER IX

MARY AND "UNCLE SAM"

Though Mary did not live long enough to vote, she participated actively in politics. She was an avid Democrat, despite her admiration for Lincoln.

A glimpse of her attitudes upon issues and personalities in the Reconstruction Era may be gleaned from an interview with a correspondent of a Washington newspaper. Speculating upon the possibility of a women's political party, he asked Mary for her qualifications for the Presidency, if the party should offer her the nomination. With an obvious air of satisfaction she declared that she possessed four qualifications for the office:

"First, if elected, I think I can make an intelligent speech of fifteen minutes when usage and the circumstances may require it, without being held up and prompted [an obvious blast at President Grant]. Second, I can entertain my guests without strangling them by the fumes of a cigar puffed in their faces [Grant again!]. Third, I have no army of relatives to fasten upon the government, to draw out its life-blood in the shape of high salaries for all kinds of useful or useless duties [Grant and his relatives]. Fourth, I have no taste whatever for gold speculations for robbing the Treasury [Grant's brother-in-law, and Jay Gould, and Black Friday]."

Turning from personalities to issues, she deplored the expenditure of $7,000,000 "for the ice crags of Alaska," and other large sums upon explorations, a new castle for the State Department, exotic but costly botanical gardens, monuments and paintings to adorn the capital. She was equally critical of Grant's obsession to annex Santo Domingo with its debts, war, and crime. Would the nation, she asked, fritter away her millions while sacred obligations in pensions to her bravest soldiers and suffering women remained uncanceled?[1]

While her principal residence remained in Washington Mary had relatively few opportunities to engage in politics except as a

105

lecturer and a lobbyist, but once she came to spend months of most years in Oswego Town she was surprisingly active, despite the obvious disadvantage of being a disfranchised female.

She participated in local caucuses, and in state and even national conventions. She also declared her candidacy for office on at least two occasions. In 1881, for example, she announced herself as a candidate for the United States Senate, and listed among her qualifications a brain which was not numbed by drugs, liquor, or tobacco. In 1890, she declared herself a candidate for Congress. Local Democrats were cool to the proposal, but the Republican press was delighted. It could think of nothing more embarrassing to the Democrats than to have the eccentric doctor poll more votes than the regular party nominee.

In May, 1892, she attended the Democratic State Convention at Syracuse with the Oswego County contingent. The Republican paper reported that her "customary manly bearing made her the cynosure of all eyes." During the meeting she sat with the Oswego delegation, an animated spectator, and joined in the applause with a flourish of her tall silk hat.[2]

A few weeks later she called a caucus at the City Hall, Oswego, to obtain "public indorsement" (including financial backing) as a delegate to the National Democratic Convention at Chicago. The Republican *Times* forecast a large turn out, but did not report the meeting. It would appear that she obtained a partial commitment from party leaders for her transportation, but that it was not immediately forthcoming; and the same paper facetiously sketched her quest, including long vigils at doorsteps and in waiting rooms, and a descent upon the office of the *Palladium*, the Democratic newspaper, while the besieged sought stratagems to dodge her. Her problem was accentuated by the state-wide division in the party ranks between the Cleveland and [Governor David B.] Hill factions. Mary was outspoken in her support of Cleveland, and therefore unacceptable to the Hillites. At the last moment, however, she appeared at the railroad station, where she advised reporters that she endorsed harmony in the party, and "planked down a fifty-dollar greenback and got her ticket to Chicago." No account of her role at the convention appears to have survived.[3]

With Cleveland in the White House Mary expressed a desire to be postmaster at Oswego, but party chiefs paid little attention to her wishes.

In the McKinley-Bryan, free-silver—gold-standard contest of 1896, Mary got off to a slow start because of her absorption in the settlement of Walker properties in Massachusetts and a round of lectures there, but she eventually gave enthusiastic allegiance to free silver and the youthful Bryan.

One of her contributions to the campaign was a ditty, sung to the tune of "Rally 'Round the Flag, Boys."

> Democrats and People's Party, wisely united—
>   Equality with all promoting.
> Justice at the White House with Bryan is now sighted—
>   Be confirmed by November's voting.
>
> Then soon prosperity will 'round our Nation hover,
>   Our Bryan all factions controlling.
> Then no transactions will be under secret cover,
>   Silver will to toilers be rolling.[4]

The score and lyrics do not seem to blend, and it is doubtful that it had any bearing upon the outcome of the election!

In 1898, Mary was again caught up in the political controversy accompanying the annexation of Hawaii. She was outraged at the callous way in which the United States deposed Queen Lilioukalani, and urged that the outraged Queen be permitted to state her case before the Senate of the United States. To circulate her views she published a pamphlet, entitled *Isonomy*, in which she rejected the American occupation of the islands as a civilizing force, and charged that the Hawaiians were more literate than her fellow countrymen. It would not appear, however, that it was imperialism, per se, which agitated the veteran reformer, but the slighting of a female. It is doubtful whether she would have risen to the defense if Queen Lil had been a Polynesian king![5]

Mary joined local Oswego Democrats again in 1900 to support Bryan for a second try for the Presidency. His stand against Republican imperialism, of course, was particularly appealing to Mary. When the Great Commoner toured Central New York in October, she went to Syracuse to greet him. She heard the silver-tongued orator from a seat on the platform, and later talked with him briefly. She then returned to Oswego to be on hand to welcome him a second time when he arrived there a day later.

Mary's penchant for blurting out whatever was on her mind, regardless of the consequences, involved her in an unfortunate incident a few days after President McKinley's death by an assassin's bullet on September 14, 1901. As she awaited a train at the railroad depot in Oswego to take her to Furniss Station (the closest station to Bunker Hill), she declared in a voice audible for some distance that if the State of New York electrocuted the President's assassin it would be committing murder, and that McKinley too was a murderer, having been responsible for the slaying of hundreds of Filipinos.

With the nation mourning its martyred President, her remarks were ill-timed, if not intemperate and in questionable taste. They can only be explained in the light of her opposition to capital punishment.

She was at once confronted by a circle of irate workmen, several of whom threatened her with bodily harm. One declared that if she were not a woman he would give her a sound beating, and a second shouted, "You are in the same class as Carrie Nation [the hatchet-wielding temperance crusader] and Emma Goldman [Russian-born anarchist]. You all ought to be put out of the way." According to the local press, a peace-maker intervened to advise that they pay no further attention to her. "She is crazy."[6]

Some years later it was reported that this incident resulted in an investigation into Mary's loyalty. An unidentified hearer, unacquainted with the Doctor's antics, reported the incident to Washington, and suggested that her pension be withdrawn. The Justice Department sent an investigator, who checked with the Oswego police. The latter gave him a briefing on Mary's peculiarities, noting that she habitually expressed her opinions in public without restraint. The agent returned to Washington, and the case was closed.[7]

Mary's loyalty to the Democratic Party militated against any enthusiasm which she might otherwise have felt for the colorful Teddy Roosevelt. Returning from a visit to Washington in the spring of 1904, she declared that the nation was in a deplorable state, that many of the Congressmen were in their dotage, and that the President was unworthy of passing notice.[8]

With another Presidential election in the offing, she resolved to attend the Democratic National Convention in St. Louis. To give her presence a semblance of regularity, and also to facilitate her financial arrangements, she called a caucus of the party. According to the local Republican sheet seven delegates and five newspaper reporters showed up. Mary opened the meeting, "and rambled and rambled through a speech while the 'delegates' one by one left the room. As the tones of her sharp, shrill voice ceased to be heard, the 'delegates' again resumed their seats and proceeded to business." They talked over the various presidential hopefuls, and then elected Mary as the "extra alternate for the New York State Delegation," without instructions, a title which was purely honorary. One committee was named to prepare credentials for her, and a second, to raise $20 for her carfare. She was off for St. Louis a few days later. Now, seventy-two, it appears to have been one of her last forays into the political arena.[9]

During the many years of her crusade for woman's rights Mary was engaged in an almost ceaseless struggle, also, for a pension. During the war she had sustained an injury to her eyes, resulting in partial muscular atrophy. She attributed it to her privation while incarcerated in Castle Thunder, but whatever its cause, the disability did not respond to treatment. It was painful, and required her to wear glasses.

At the time of her discharge from the service she was awarded $8.50 per month for this injury, beginning on June 13, 1865. The small grant simply stimulated her desire for more, and she joined in the scramble for a pension.

She had plenty of company. Prior to 1890 such an award required an act of Congress. Members of that body introduced thousands of requests for their constituents, most of which eventually died in committee, depending in part on the current finances of the government, the persuasiveness of the interested Congressman, and sometimes, at least, upon the merits of the case and the persistence of the applicant. Beginning in 1872 Mary launched an annual campaign for such an act.

In an interview with a reporter of the *Washington Daily Chronicle* concerning her work for nurses' pensions, she was asked, "What about your own bill? I hear you always work for others and leave yourself last; but everybody seems to think that you will be successful. The press and the people say it is a just claim, and that it will surely pass."

Mary's response was tactful, a rather rare phenomenon. The

members of Congress had been kind and deferential toward her, she replied, and she believed they were honest. No other country in the world would have delayed justice so long, but she declared that she would overlook it. She had apologized while in Europe for her country's failure to appropriate a sum for her "befitting its boasted greatness and justness." If again postponed, "Another year may find me where no earthly justice will avail me, and then, not only the present Congress in their military committee, would forever feel thorns in their pillows, but future generations would censure them, until their children's children would disown any relationship." The press of business would not serve as an excuse, she insisted, when larger amounts were being voted for monuments for dead men, and hospitality for foreigners. But the Congressmen, presumably, were not troubled about the condemnation of their descendants, and her bill died in committee.[10]

But for Mary there was another year of earthly justice and another pension bill. The *Congressional Globe* and the *Congressional Record* leave no doubts as to her tenacity in this matter. In a period of thirty years, at least twenty-five bills were introduced in the House and Senate in her behalf.

One of her early petitions, dated March 6, 1873, and written in her hand, is in the files of the Pension Bureau. In it she stressed her "assidious labors," in behalf of the sick and wounded, and her disability, which permitted her to perform the duties of her profession only to a limited degree. During her captivity, she averred, she had suffered from an inadequate diet, which impaired her sight, so that she could read but a few lines in a newspaper.

She claimed that General Schenck, currently the United States Minister to England, had asked her in 1866 whether she would accept a pension of $25 per month for life. She declared that she had refused, believing that the impairment of her vision was only temporary.

Now, however, she found that she could not live in the North in winter because of the brightness of the sun upon the snow; nor could she face the hot humid climate of the South in summer. Required to move from place to place, she could not practice medicine to any extent, and was deprived of a means of comfortable support. She also found that she had to rest her eyes more frequently; that when riding and at meetings, both day and night, she was forced to sit with her eyes closed much of the time.

She tossed a testimonial to dress reform into her plea, observing that she was "able to sit up a great part of the time during the warm weather by being dressed in the least burdensome manner, that is, without petticoats or other bands or burdens dragging upon her spine."

She concluded with a request for a monthly pension of $24, and with a reminder that she had no real or personal property except what was usual for a medical practitioner, and no horse or carriage.

In time, Mary's quest became almost legendary. Newspapers in the 1880s and 1890s, for example, reported that she was deprived of a grant of $15,000 which a grateful House of Representatives had earmarked for her outstanding services in the medical department of the army, and which the Senate had accepted with the proviso that "her benevolence would lead her to use the greater portion of it in reporting to friends of those who died at Andersonville, as she had also been a prisoner of war." But the "sharp practice" of some members of Congress had prevented her from obtaining the award, and it had gone to some other woman. There is no evidence of such an appropriation in the records of Congress.[11]

Details of her perennial search for a pension become tedious, and need not be repeated. Such was not the case, however, in the following instance:

In 1872 she sought $10,000 for services rendered without compensation and for money which she expended for the sick and wounded. When it was reported that her petition had been rejected because of her unorthodox clothing, she drafted a set of resolutions proposing an amendment to the Constitution to provide for a national costumer to be selected from a foreign court, and authorized to devise costumes for all American women including squaws. The biting sarcasm and flare for comedy which exude from the document warrant its reproduction.

> Whereas, Word has been sent me that the reason why my bill of $10,000 has not been paid by the present session of the United States Congress is because I do not dress like other women notwithstanding the fact that

111

there is no national costumer elected or appointed under existing laws; and

Whereas, The Constitution of the United States has made no provision for such an important personage; and

Whereas, Under such constitution the liberty of limbs and vital organs is included in the rights and liberties that are guaranteed regardless of sex; and

Whereas, An amendment to the constitution must be had in order to curtail a woman's right to relieve herself of the burden and undue expense of the covering considered essential in civilized nations; and

Whereas, The American squaws dress so that they can not be distinguished from the Indians; and

Whereas, The vulgarity of woman dressing like a man should exclude squaws from the annual per capita amount appropriated by the United States Congress; and

Whereas, The cut of garments for women is not considered to be in any style unless they are designed by foreigners, as Americans are not competent to devise what is paramount in importance to every consideration in life, viz., health, comfort, convenience, economy of cloth and economy of brain in devising ever-changing styles that are so important in tariff considerations; the right of petition which such petitioner conceives to be in her interest is the inalienable right of an American citizen, therefore she asks that the following bill be passed as one of the graceful acts of the Fifty-first United States Congress:

Be it enacted by the Senate and House of Representatives in Congress assembled; that the Constitution of the United States be amended so as to read: That a national costumer for the women of the United States be selected from some foreign court whose special duties shall be to devise costumes for every woman in the United States and territories that shall seem appropriate to him and that this act includes squaws as well as other women.

Be it further enacted, etc., that whoever disregards

the fashion plates in a national magazine published by said costumer shall have no appropriation from the government of the United States and their men relatives shall be debarred from pensions and appropriations during the life time of such women.

And be it further enacted that the salary of such costumer shall be $10,000 per year, and the magazine published at the government office once in three months and sent to every woman in the United States free of expense.[12]

There can be no doubt that the resolutions eased the pain of the lost pension.

Mary subsequently pared down the sum requested, but her petitions remained unanswered. But in the end, perseverance paid off. In 1890 the Harrison administration accepted a general law to cover all veterans who could not do physical labor. And eight years later Mary won her battle. At the age of sixty-six she was awarded $20 a month, including the $8.50 which she received since 1865. Though small, it came in time to ease the financial burdens of her declining years.[13]

It is interesting to note that while Mary was striving for a pension, she was shocked by what she considered to be fraudulent claims. On one occasion she broadcast a list of beneficiaries, whom she labeled undeserving, and branded as "conspirators." She went so far as to intercede to prevent her brother Alvah from obtaining a pension, but he got it just the same!

Mary was not content to simply harry Congress for a pension. Upon her withdrawal from the front line of the suffrage campaign, she set her sights upon a position in one of the Federal departments in Washington. She first singled out the Treasury Department, and in 1873 obtained a recommendation from the Treasurer of the United States, Francis E. Spinner, who had been the first public official to advocate the employment of women in the governmental services. He wrote that Mary was competent and deserving, and worthy of a favorable consideration on the basis of her war service.

Mary appeared before the chief clerk of the appointment office, answered routine questions satisfactorily, and took the usual oath to support the Constitution. She was then ordered to report to

Mr. Spinner, who directed her to a clerk to outline her duties. But for reasons unexplained her appointment was not signed by the Secretary of the Treasury, W. A. Richardson. Assuming that only red tape was responsible, Mary appeared at the office day after day, and month after month. She later testified that she had maintained this daily vigil for two years without an assignment, and of course without pay.

She finally abandoned hope of an appointment, and petitioned Congress for redress, asking for $900, a year's pay. The Assistant Secretary of the Treasury, Henry F. French, investigated her case, and ruled that she was not entitled to compensation. But Mary persisted, and had the case reopened. The Solicitor General of the Treasury, at length, reported that she was badly treated. She was promised a position by the Treasurer, was examined and declared competent, and told to report. This, he held, was tantamount to appointment, and the formal signing of her employment by the Secretary of the Treasury was not required. He accepted Mary's sworn statement that she had refused other professional positions during the two-year period, and recommended that she be paid the $900 requested.

The Committee of Claims of the House of Representatives accepted the Solicitor General's report, and prepared a bill to implement it. Noting that no justification of her treatment had been forthcoming from the Treasury Department, it speculated upon her "well known peculiarities of dress and manner." They might have been considered in both an appointment and dismissal, but could not justify shabby treatment. Despite the favorable report, however, Mary was never compensated for her troubles.[14]

The defeat did not dim her ardor for a governmental career. She simply waited until Hayes replaced Grant in the White House, and then renewed her assault upon the new Administration. With the support of her local Congressman, she bombarded the Secretary of the Interior, Carl Schurz, with letters from Oswego's prominent politicians and added, for good measure, notices of her books collected from the journals. She failed again, but four years later, in 1881, there was still another Administration, that of Garfield, and another bid for office. Her prospects remained dim, however, until an assassin's bullet vaulted Chester A. Arthur, a New York politician, into the Presidency. Six months later, in April, 1882, she had the satisfaction of an appointment as a clerk in the mailroom of the Pensions Office of the Department of the Interior. Her work was clerical and routine, but as will be seen, it did not remain so in her hands.

A regular income, after more than a decade of improvising, was a tonic to the new civil servant. Perley Poore, dean of Washington correspondents, observed Mary at this time at President Arthur's first New Year's Day Reception in 1882. She was "the observed of all observers," as she came "tripping in with elastic step." She shook hands with President Arthur with obvious relish and a patter of words and passed down the line, nodding to the wives of the dignitaries. In her black broadcloth frock coat and pantaloons, tall silk hat and slender cane she was a vision of sartorial splendor, whatever spectators might have thought of her taste. She moved from the Blue Room into the East Room as eyes and heads turned. It was noted, however, that few came forward to speak to her.[15]

During the early months in the mailroom she was accepted, with some reservations to be sure, by her fellow employees, and the atmosphere seems to have been friendly. She later affirmed that she was "sought to give prescriptions and loan small sums of money, and do little offices of kindness that I *invariably* responded to."[16] The chief of the mailroom, D. L. Gitt, who later became critical of Mary's performance, conceded that "at first she promised better things."[17] But the honeymoon was brief.

Ten months after her appointment the assistant to the chief of the mailroom referred to her as "a firebrand in our midst, insulting to the ladies and inattentive to her duties as clerk, spending her time in writing private correspondence." He seldom gave her assignments, he complained, because it raised a fuss. She would refuse them, insisting that she was unable to do the work. "In justice to the mailroom," he urged that she be transferred to another part of the office. Having had to suffer with her for most of a year, "someone else ought to bear their share of the burden."[18]

Mary's version of the deterioration of relations and those given by her superiors in the office are so much at variance that they are impossible to reconcile. But there was no doubt that she was a center of controversy.

She charged that there was a conspiracy among employees of the mailroom to have her dismissed, and that their hostility toward her stemmed from her resolve to correct abuses which she had uncovered, and her insistence that the work be done promptly and correctly.

Chief Gitt, by contrast, maintained that Mary had "diligently avoided every kind of work, pleading a new excuse for each kind of labor assigned." She had first complained of her eyes, then her chest, then her right arm, and finally her left arm. She was "violent, high tempered and abusive," and "aggressive and insolent," conduct calculated to destroy the obedience of the division. He further charged that she spent much of her time reading newspapers and doing her own personal work, and that she ate and slept at her desk during office hours. When she accepted an assignment, her work was frequently incorrect. She had objected to the location of her desk, the lighting, and temperature. They had attempted to accommodate her, but without success. Maintenance personnel had learned to stay clear of her, and he had attempted to regulate the windows and window shades himself, without success. He also charged excessive absence. In a period of one year she had missed 112 days, little of which she had spent in bed.[19]

A complaint by Jere Haralson, a Negro employed in the office, was added to the case against her. He alleged that in the presence of others in the division, she had called him "a dirty, stinking Nigger," and that she had done so without cause. He had always tried to do his duty, he declared, and should not be insulted because he was a colored man.[20]

Mary's dismissal was contemplated by the management of the mail division in May, 1883, but they seem to have hesitated to face the consequences. Early in June she applied for five weeks sick leave, and received a verbal approval. But hearing a rumor that she would be relieved of her duties, she remained on the job until her request was signed and included the date for her return. Meanwhile, on June 8, she forwarded a request for transfer to the position of special examiner in the Pension Division. With her sick leave, and also a rating report of her performance of duty, a recent innovation in the Interior Department in hand, she left Washington for her home in Oswego.

Action in Washington followed quickly. Chief Gitt recommended Mary's dismissal to W. W. Dudley, Commissioner of the Pension Division, and the latter forwarded it with his endorsement to H. M. Teller, the Secretary of the Interior. Days later at

Oswego Mary received a notification of discharge from Secretary Teller with a short explanation that there were no appropriations to continue her position.

Mary's counter-attack was both instantaneous and spirited. She shot back a defense of her conduct to the Deputy Commissioner, citing her rating report as evidence of competency. He passed it along to Commissioner Dudley, who, sensing that he was in for a fight, dispatched another note to Secretary Teller, advising him that a restoration of Mary to office would be prejudicial to the service.

Early on the morning of July 19, following the expiration of her sick leave on July 18, Mary was at the office door of the mailroom to claim her job, but she was refused admittance. She proceeded to the office of Commissioner Dudley, only to be told that his whereabouts were unknown. She waited, but he did not appear. That evening she went to his house, and after a long delay was admitted by his wife. The latter protested that the Commissioner was not at home, but Mary held her ground until she was satisfied that he was, in reality, out of the city.

She eventually tracked him down and obtained a hearing. In addition to the allegations listed above, Chief Gitt now charged that Mary was lazy, and that she had talked disrespectfully of the late President Garfield.

Mary's defense was a ringing denial of at least most of the charges. She pointed to the ratings of the personnel to demonstrate her competence. On punctuality she stood above the departmental average, and on accuracy, she was just below it. She was substantially below the median on industry and rapidity, but her over-all score on the five criteria: punctuality, industry, rapidity, habits and accuracy, was not significantly lower than the mean; and based upon a point system of seven for a perfect performance and zero for complete deficiency, Mary's score was 5.80; the departmental average, 6.73. It would appear that either the complaints of her incompetency were exaggerated, or the scoring system was invalid.[21]

She admitted that she ate at her desk. It was her custom to come early, well in advance of the opening hour. Between nine and ten o'clock she took a few minutes to eat a cold lunch. She ate only what was required to live and to do her work correctly, and thereby avoid suffering among the pensioners from unnecessary delays. She closed her eyes briefly when they pained her, and she looked at newspapers for a few moments only when she was not busy.

It might be noted that clerical work undoubtedly placed a strain upon her defective vision. She scorned to answer the accusation that she was lazy. It was ridiculous, and completely inconsistent with another claim that she "was doing something all the time."[22]

Again, evidence would appear to support Mary. Whatever her shortcomings, she was not lazy.

To a charge that her "aggressive manners had lost the personal regard of every one," she retorted that her associations had been friendly until she had made her position clear that the work must be correct, and that she would not sanction errors and delays.

It did not seem to occur to her that a clerk might not have been expected to assume responsibility for the entire Pensions Service.

She acknowledged that she had no active friends in the office, but declared that she did not go into the office for its social benefits. She had simply pursued the even tenor of business as well as she could.

She denied that her absences had been excessive, claiming that they had all been legal. She had been ill during the entire period, she insisted, except for three weeks when she had visited her sick mother.

She denied Haralson's charge that she had made disparaging remarks regarding his color; but admitted saying that "President Arthur was a grand exchange for Garfield, as much as an assassination was to be deplored."

At this point Mary took the offensive, charging that letters from pension seekers marked "personal," were read in the mailroom rather than passed directly to the Commissioner.[23]

Finding that Commissioner Dudley was not inclined to reverse his position after her two-hour defense, she drew up her version of the hearing and forwarded it to Secretary Teller. She held that the conspirators came with malice aforethought, and were guilty of wily moves, and studied schemes. They had condemned her without an opportunity to call witnesses, upon *ex parte* evidence.

Meanwhile, in his report to Secretary Teller, Commissioner Dudley recommended that her dismissal stand.

118

Refusing to accept her discharge as final, Mary now pulled out all of the stops. She charged that two of the principal conspirators, Gitt and a Mrs. Druce, had been meeting illicitly at the office in the mornings before office hours, and that she had twice found them in a compromising position in a closet just a few yards from Gitt's desk. She also alleged that Commissioner Dudley had ordered a clerk to make disabilities on a pension application, when a clerk had found none. She called upon Secretary Teller to dismiss him. To add weight to her charges she swore to their veracity before a Justice of the Peace.[24]

Unwilling to make the final decision in Mary's case, Secretary Teller requested the Assistant Attorney General, Joseph K. McCammon, to review the conflicting testimony. He, in turn, reported that after a full consideration he was unable to conclude that Dr. Walker had been a victim of any conspiracy in the Pension Office. Thwarted again, Mary went directly to President Arthur, claiming that McCammon was either incompetent or was influenced by reasons not made apparent in the decision.

There is no evidence that Arthur reopened the case.

The dismissal proceedings had dragged on from July into November, and in the process Mary had poured forth a voluminous defense filling some 150 pages. But it availed her nought.

After a sobering reappraisal, she attempted to salvage monetary compensation from her misadventure. She compiled the sum which she would have received from her dismissal date to the end of the year, and sent claims for it to the proper authorities, including the Secretary of the Interior. It was rejected. A year later she requested a reopening of the entire case. It was also declined. Thus ended Mary's career as a government servant.

Mary's fleeting connection with the mail may have had lasting effects upon the efficiency of the service. She subsequently took credit for devising a postcard receipt for registered letters, and also for a law which permitted senders to place their names and addresses on the wrappers. These claims have been repeated many times, including the *Dictionary of American Biography*.[25] Records in the Post Office Department show that the return card with registered mail was adopted in 1879, at a time Mary was in Washington, but two years prior to her regular employment in the Pension Office. The records do not identify the inventor.[26]

Removed from her post in the Department of the Interior, and without immediate prospect for a pension, Mary took a last fling at the lecture circuit in 1887. Lacking sponsors within the suffrage movement, she obtained bookings through a professional agency, Kohl and Middleton, to appear as one of a series of acts at sideshows in dime museums. Had she been more sensitive of public opinion, she would have found the situation incongruous and even unbearable, but the indomitable little lady took it in stride and, presumably, without misgivings.

In arranging for her appearance the agents asked her for a few autobiographical statements to be used for publicity. In response, she conjured a series of catch-lines which would have done credit to a professional. For example:

> Dr. Mary E. Walker is often taken for a Clergyman, and especially at the Catholic Church, owing to her smooth face.
>
> No one can talk so plainly on social questions and command such close attention and profound respect as Dr. Mary E. Walker.
>
> Dr. Mary E. Walker was not only the most prominent woman in the United States Army, but has been the most steadily prominent of any American woman ever since that time. No woman on our soil has such a versatility of talents, and yet she is the most refined woman that is before the public, notwithstanding all of her public life among all classes of people.
>
> There is one woman alone in Washington, whom the breath of slander has never touched regarding her moral character, and she has a place in the best social circles, such as no other lone woman has, and is loved by all good people in all classes, for the bridging over of troubles for *every body*. Washington would not be Washington without our Dr. Walker.
>
> Dr. Mary E. Walker is not a giant, nor as old as Methuselah, nor as strong as Samson, and yet everybody rushes to see what she has to say about the prominent topics of the age.[27]

Whatever Kohl and Middleton's reactions may have been to Mary's self-glorification, they were willing to concede that her performances were varied, colorful, and dynamic. In rapid-fire order she delivered short lectures on topics as varied as the science of dress, woman's franchise, the labor question, the evils of tobacco, human electricity, and the curiosities of the brain. It would be interesting to know whether any patron had the endurance to pay the admission fees to hear all of the lectures. In adjacent booths the public was offered Punch and Judy shows, life-saving resuscitation, and Mexican feather workers.

Mary filled engagements of several weeks in Chicago, Cincinnati, Buffalo and Detroit, and possibly in other cities. For a week's performance she received $150, not an unattractive remuneration in an era of deflated prices, from which she paid her living expenses and transportation. Further evidence that she was not begging for survival may be found in the fact that she insisted upon a parlor or a dressing room, where she could rest between performances. She also refused to appear in a hall which reeked with poisonous tobacco. Kohl and Middleton reassured her that she need not fear tobacco. Wonderland [the museum in question in Detroit] was without doubt the largest and finest furnished museum in the country. She could use her own stage as her parlor fitted out with a couch and other furnishings; or she might use the ladies' parlors.[28]

Her tour, with occasional open dates, extended from October through January. The following fall she performed in similar houses in Detroit and Buffalo. And again, in 1893, when sixty-one, she filled bookings in Toledo and New York. In Toledo the local press reported her act with the heading:

DR. MARY WALKER

From the Platform of Princes to the Stage of Freaks

The article continued: "Dr. Mary Walker will be at Wonderland all next week. There was a time when this remarkable woman stood upon the same platform as Presidents and the world's greatest women. There is something grotesque in her appearance on the stage built for freaks." Other features in the Curio Hall included: Captain Sydney Hinman, captain of the life-saving crew at Coney Island, with his complete life-saving outfit; Professor Stendell with his experiments in electricity; the

Mexican feather workers; and Stephen Stephens and his London Punch and Judy show.[29]

In New York at the Vine Street Dime Museum she lectured on dress, with particular emphasis upon the impracticability of crinoline. When spread over hoops on the hips, the tiny Doctor alleged, its constant swaying caused nervous afflictions. And when worn on stairways and while getting into or out of street cars, it offered inadequate protection; in fact it was decidedly immoral. It was wholly unsuited to rapid transit: "Ten women will fill up a car; men will be tripped up; and all sorts of trouble will follow if hoopskirts become the fashion."[30]

In exposing the incompatibility of hoops and modern transportation, Mary was on the right track. In fact, she almost witnessed a break-through for dress reform at this time, though it was not street cars as much as bicycles which provided the impetus.

Long, flowing skirts, and least of all hoops, were impracticable for bicycling, and the wheel was popular with women as well as men. By 1895, the bloomer and the divided skirt were occasionally in view on the highways, and were being heralded as marking woman's emancipation. Mary's work in performing the spadework was apparent. The *Albany Argus,* for example, devoted two columns to a new dress on exhibit in Paris with a divided skirt to permit bicycling. "Dr. Mary Walker, long laughed at," it observed, "has lived to see her sisters follow her example. . . . Half a century ago it made a woman [Mary] famous as a standard almanac joke." The new fad, it predicted, was masculine enough to satisfy "good Dr. Mary Walker's taste." She had argued for pants, it continued, and had suffered for it, for the practice had caught on only in the gymnasium and on the stage until this moment, when "its day of fate was ripe."[31]

It turned out that the forecast was a bit premature. The bicycle proved to be but the entering wedge for the reform. Its more complete fulfillment would await the coming of the twentieth century and the horseless carriage.

Chapter X

OSWEGO TOWN'S LITTLE DYNAMO

During the late 1880s and early 1890s Mary spent less time in Washington and made Oswego the base of her operations, though it could scarcely be called her home until the turn of the century. Several years before the death of her father in 1880, she received title to the farm in Oswego Town, upon the condition that one-half of its annual income should go to her mother during her life. It was not an unmixed blessing, since the farm was encumbered by a mortgage of $1,000. She also assumed the obligation of looking after her mother, now eighty and in failing health, a responsibility hardly compatible with her frequent and prolonged absences.[1]

Misunderstandings between Mary and her mother and her brother, Alvah, quickly followed. Her mother complained that she could not remain in the house during Mary's absences, and took up her residence with Alvah, who lived next door. And when Alvah, possibly to compensate himself for the care of his mother, stabled his horses in Mary's barn, she turned them into the road. Alvah seems to have taken preliminary steps to contest his father's will, but reconsidered. For several years thereafter, Mary and Alvah avoided each other, though living side by side.

Mary's management of her farm was also beset with misunderstandings. Either she selected tenants who were incompetent and unsuited to rural life, or her incessant prying into their affairs drove them from the premises. Letters from a tenant, a physician who had previously resided in Washington, in 1882, graphically illustrate the plight of a victim caught in her web.

I have a copy of our contract before me which reads that I "agree not to entertain patients or boarders *now at a distance* from there without the consent of Dr. Walker," which upsets all your argument about "a fair and square bargain not to have any patients this year."

Our agreement entitles me to take all the patients and boarders we wish who may be in this vicinity. . . . If you refuse to allow [a patient from a distance], he may come as a visitor, as has any of our friends. . . .

You must remember that we did not hang around your place soliciting an opportunity to come up to this delightful neighborhood, but that it was all *your own doing, our coming here,* and that *we objected* in all reasonable ways except in a positive *no*, which we have regretted many times we did not give as an answer, but having been drawn into the trap and at such a loss and at such an expense to our slim purses, we intend to make the most of our opportunities. . . .

As to furnishing my friend's name to you, for you to dissect in our absence, I shall do no such thing.[2]

The tenant then got down to particulars: the lack of fences, stock, tools and machinery; in all, a diatribe requiring some eleven closely written pages. Needless to say, the tenancy had an early termination. The experience did not deter her from trying again.

She continued to have difficulties in the management of the farm when she resided upon it, and depended upon neighbors to do the farming. On one occasion she refused to allow Charles Peck, who had cut hay on shares, to remove his portion until lumber and harness, which she alleged had been stolen, were returned. Peck sued her for slander. In the trial the plaintiff's attorney sought to ruffle her by asking questions of an embarrassing nature: Her age? and was she ever married? Both questions at first elicited indignant refusals, but after conferring with her counsel she complied. "I am perfectly willing after a long life of rectitude to say I am sixty years old"; and to the second, "I have reconsidered, I was married."

Attorney for the plaintiff: "How long ago?"

Mary: "I have almost forgotten."

Attorney: "What was his name?"

Mary: "It was in November, 1855; his name was Surgeon Miller. I have never gone by the name of Miller."

A verdict of $50 was eventually awarded to the plaintiff. Mary's attorney made a motion for a new trial, but she did not press it.[3]

But there was more to come. A few evenings later Mary delivered a lecture in the special term room of the court house for the purpose of raising the $50, and an additional $80 for costs. The audience was sparse, and the sum collected small. But Mary gave a full-length performance. She voiced her version of the controversy with Peck, and added her analysis of diphtheria, tuberculosis, and the effects of tobacco upon the lungs. A reporter, who covered the meeting, declared that he was soon "fogged in an avalanche of cachexia, neurataxia, taxemia, neurotics, seveora ganglia, and cerebellum medulla oblongata."[4]

Many years later a daughter of Judge Merrick Stowell, who presided over the Peck *vs* Walker trial, recalled that, while the case was before the court, Dr. Mary Walker called at their home to see her father. Finding that he was out of the house, she told her version of the disagreement to his daughter, charging that she was being persecuted. Lest her visit should come to nought, Mary wrote a note of explanation to the judge, and entrusted it to her young hostess. Later, when the judge returned, and was given the message by his unsuspecting daughter, he fell into a towering rage, and swore that he would not be influenced. He tore up the missive without reading it.

Several years later, the situation was reversed: Mary initiated court action to collect what she considered to be her share of the produce. But despite her impassioned presentation, the verdict went to the defendants.[5]

A check on Mary's movements during the 1890s reveals that she averaged about six months a year in Oswego. Her arrivals and departures fell into no particular pattern, except for her trips to Washington, which usually corresponded to the sessions of Congress. On other occasions, she was off to New Hampshire and Massachusetts, to thrust herself into a murder trial in the former, and to contest an aunt's will in the latter. In between times, she lived upon her oft-neglected farm, fitting her labors to the season at hand.

This, of course, left much to be desired; she made arrangements for planting and harvesting and lesser details hastily, inviting disagreements later. During this decade no farmer remained in her employ for more than a single season, and at least five of her tenants went to court with grievances. Mary's evaluation of her rustic paradise seems to have been colored by her affection for the place, or perhaps she simply misrepresented it. In any event, the relationship ended in disillusionment.

It would be misleading to assume that there was a typical year on the farm; but after the crops had been divided according to plan, Mary could anticipate enough hay and straw to feed and bed her livestock, consisting of a horse and cow, and a few bushels of oats for the chickens and an occasional bonus for her undernourished steed. Mary churned her own butter, and carried the surplus to the store. She also had apples in sufficient supply to provide several barrels of vinegar, which she sold in small lots, and enough walnuts for petty sales or gifts. She supplied her own table with potatoes, green corn, turnips, and other garden vegetables. The yield in produce and money permitted a Spartan existence, but left little or nothing for taxes and maintenance. The farm was deteriorating, and it is doubtful whether she could have retained it, had not her sister, Aurora Walker Coats, stepped into the breach.

Seven years older than Mary, and the widow of a prosperous farmer, Lyman Coats, Aurora was both a shrewd manager and a kindly neighbor. When negotiating a contract for the rental of her fields, she was all business, but when there was misfortune, folks sent for Mrs. Coats. She seldom set out for town in her carriage or on foot without a basket of eatables from her well-stocked pantry for distribution en route; and her friends saw to it that she did not return empty handed.

A similar childhood environment and a few years of school teaching at the Tallman district school nearby produced in Aurora a self-reliance and rugged independence second only to that of her sister. Instead of studying medicine, she married and became a mother. But farm work did not preclude broader interests—phrenology, for example. She devoured the current journals on this science and practiced the art of head-reading when opportunity knocked: at a Fulton hotel, while atte.ding the county fair, in a grocery store in Oswego, or in her living room. She also spoke before the local literary society at the Cobblestone School on child training, flower and berry growing, and other assorted subjects. At the county and town fairs, where her husband had exhibited blooded cattle, she garnered awards for her canned fruits and needlework. Unlike Mary, she was an avid church goer; but her Presbyterianism did not prevent her from an active association with the Methodists at Oswego Center and the Baptists at Southwest Oswego.

For Mary, Aurora had a sympathetic and abiding understanding, which the former's eccentricities failed to shatter. Her affection was reciprocated by Mary, and the sisters seem never to have had a serious misunderstanding. When Mary accepted an invitation to speak from the stage of a dime museum, Aurora was not shocked. Instead, her reaction was the thrill of commanding $150 a week![6]

When Mary came home after a prolonged absence, Aurora saw to it that there were foodstuffs and kindling on hand, and through the days which followed she was a frequent visitor bearing a variety of berries and fruits from her garden, and baked goods from her kitchen. It was not a one-way street, however; Aurora's basket was seldom empty when she trudged the two miles homeward. It might be green corn, apples or potatoes, or more frequently produce which grew on the farm without cultivation: cowslips, huckleberries, May apples or walnuts. Mary also made her horse and buggy available to Aurora, when the Coats' horses were needed in the fields; and when Aurora was ill she nursed her, laundered her clothes, and helped with the chores.

But Aurora was more essential to Mary than vice versa. Once, Aurora extricated Mary from a lawsuit by going over her head to arrange a settlement out of court; again, she drew up an agreement for the payment of a note for $50, which Mary owed to a sister-in-law, by transferring the former's cow to the latter, and advancing the balance herself. It should not be assumed, however, that Aurora simply paid Mary's bills. She did not; but she straightened out many snarls in Mary's tangled finances.

If Mary's arrival in Oswego touched off a chain of favors from Aurora, her departure sometimes required even greater sacrifices. Mary frequently set off on her journeys on short notice, leaving a host of problems. Aurora supplied the cash for her railroad fare and, having seen her off at the station, went back to the farm to close the house. When winter came, she dragged the vegetables to the cellar to avoid freezing and, on one occasion during an exceptional cold-snap, poured water on the cellar floor to moderate the frosty temperature (a farm trick new to this writer!). For some weeks during one winter Aurora virtually lived on the Walker farm to take care of the livestock left unattended at

Mary's unexpected exodus. The seventy-year-old matriarch tended the wood stove, fed the horse and cow, cleaned the stables, replaced broken windows, and even entertained the neighbors while keeping her vigil in the lonely old house.

When Aurora wrote her will, it was Mary who was uppermost in her mind. "To my sister, Mary E. Walker, M.D.," she wrote, "who is the poorest of my sisters, my bay horse Barney, harness and red horse blanket, and my new stove, The Good Morning, with a suggestion that she sell her horse, Dolly; and all she owes me is cancelled in consideration of her help in sickness and health. One of my diaries, tea kettles with covers, and a pancake griddle."[7]

Four years after drafting the original document, Aurora crossed out the line reading "and all she owes me is cancelled," and wrote over it, "This has been paid, 1898." A year later she added, "I will my buggy to Dr. Walker."

It might be noted that the "Good Morning" stove had been replaced by a newer model, and the horse, Fred, sold some time before Aurora's demise, so that Mary did not receive these mementos. Incidentally, Aurora willed that her goods be divided among her two grandsons, "if they do not drink, smoke tobacco, and swear."

Mary's security in her declining years appears to have troubled Aurora in her last months. When her daughter, Vesta, scolded her for inviting Mary into her home, Aurora reacted in her diary: "Dr. W. fetched me and my meat home. She gave me some candy. Vesta and Charles [Fenske, her husband] were angry about Dr. coming in, just as if it was any of their business." And in another entry a few days earlier, she observed that Mary had given her "8 nice pears and 6 ears of pop corn. Dr. divides everything with me. I have always been good to her. May God bless her in her old age, and may she never want for bread or anything else."[8]

On the morning of May 13, 1900, while working in her kitchen, Aurora collapsed and expired. The coroner attributed her death to a hemorrhage of the lungs. She was in her seventy-fifth year.

When news of Aurora's death reached Mary in Washington, she rushed home. She arrived after the funeral service was under way. A neighbor recalls that Mary entered, uninvited, and placed a small bouquet on the coffin, and that at the conclusion of the service she walked to the cemetery just a few rods down the road.

The death of Aurora in one respect was more than the loss of a sister. It was the passing of Mary's generation. As the twentieth century dawned there were few to remember her early triumphs; the new generation saw only an odd old woman clad in ridiculous clothing.

It might be added that Mary was on friendly terms also with her two other sisters, Vesta (Mrs. W. Randolph Worden), and Luna (Mrs. Wickham W. Griswold), and their children. But they lived a few miles from the Walker homestead, and were not involved in Mary's daily affairs as was Aurora. Her brothers-in-law had assisted her in job and pension hunting. They also held mortgages on her farm for sums ranging from $300 to $700.

The affection of Mary's sisters and their families, however, did not secure her younger nephews and nieces from the embarrassment of being her relatives. One niece recalls walking around a block on the way to school to avoid meeting her eccentric aunt face to face in the presence of her school friends.

As Mary began to spend more time on the farm, she dreamed of converting it into a sanatorium, or possibly a school for young women. None of her schemes ever got off the ground, but several received wide coverage in the press; and one in 1895 found its way into the newspapers of far off Australia.

The initial publicity seems to have started in England, where it may have been planted by Mary. Oswego papers copied an article from the *London Chronicle*, which reported that Dr. Walker planned an Adamless Eden on a 135-acre tract. It was to be a colony for young women who would pledge themselves to single blessedness. They would work and study, and eventually go forth as samples of the new womanhood.[9] Dozens of American papers repeated the story, and Bill Nye, the nation's favorite homespun columnist and satirist, added his touch, and passed it along to millions of readers. According to his version, the colony was to be entirely female—even roosters and turkey gobblers would be eliminated when identified. Unhappy married men would be permitted to look over the fence on stated occasions at the Eden inside, where they might witness "milkmaids in red morocco slippers, white duck trousers and white tarlatan chemisettes . . . or picturesque Maul Mullers in lavender pantses raking crab grass with rakes all gay with ribbons."[10]

Fortunately, one curious journalist, W. D. Inslee, decided to go to her farm, and get the story first-hand. His subsequent article in the December, 1895, issue of the *Metropolitan Magazine* was a fair and sympathetic recital of her plans.

She declared it to be a project which she had been formulating for many years. "Every woman must do something to be somebody. Girls who intend to marry must learn what housekeeping and household duties mean. This is especially true of women who are to become farmers' wives. My intention is to make my place a sort of training school for these women, and when desired, practical instruction in actual field work." She denied the report that bloomers were required. Girls might choose their own apparel. It would not be a "new woman's colony, but a new wives' training school."

Leaving Mary's schemes for a colony, and turning to her life, as he observed it, Inslee noted that in addition to doing most of the work on her farm, she was a jack-of-all-trades as a physician in the neighborhood. "She plays the part of dentist, surgeon and physician to all the ailing that apply to her, and she is charitable in the extreme. . . .

"Dr. Mary is now over fifty [sixty-three] years of age, but she is still robust. She has a small but excellent library, and a number of interesting relics, including a chair that was used in the White House and has been occupied by every President from Washington to the second Adams. Dr. Walker does not believe in tobacco. This is apparent the moment one enters her front door, opposite which on the wall, appears a sign in black letters bearing the inscription, 'No smoking!' . . .

"There are many more pretentious places than this old-fashioned house, but there is no place where contentment and peace are more in evidence than in Dr. Mary Walker's Colony of One."[11]

It remained a colony of one. But five years later Mary had another plan for her farm: "A Home Sanitarium School . . . for the Cure of Consumption, with a Preventive School . . . for those Susceptible to Condition Producing Consumption." She issued a broadside which emphasized her special fitness as a director, and portrayed her home as an ideal location.

"It is not on a mountain with the air rare, not in a valley with the air heavy, not on a plain with the air kept impure, not near a river with fogs; it is four and a half miles from a city—free from the noises that prevent recuperative sleep, free from the irritating smoke of cities. No railway noises are nearer than a mile, and a little station [Furniss Station] without immediate inhabitants is but little farther distant, where patients can be brought from a sleeping car in an electric carriage with ambulance facilities." What more idyllic setting could nature afford? She closed her prospectus with a ringing appeal: "At Bunker Hill, in Boston, Massachusetts, was fought a great battle in national salvation. Let us hasten to begin at Bunker Hill, Oswego, New York, individual consumptive battles for life, whose numbers shall far exceed those who fought for national salvation."[12]

Again, the public remained apathetic, and her hopes remained unfulfilled. It appears to have been her final drive to convert her spare acres into a social experiment. It did not preclude colonies of two or three, however, and the almost inevitable termination in charges and counter-charges.

Perhaps the most colorful of these was that which involved the "Princess" Frederika Nicolas. Mary had met the princess during the Civil War, when the latter was a nurse, and known simply as Eleanor Bishop; she had known her later as a reader and songstress in New York. Miss Bishop eventually married a man claiming to be a Greek prince, and settled in Rutland, Vermont. Then, in the summer of 1913, the elderly princess addressed an urgent appeal to the aging Oswego physician: "My life is in danger, and so is that of my dear friend, Miss Rheims (my faithful maid)." She begged Mary to hasten to Rutland and snatch her from "villains trying to send us to an asylum, and seize all of our property." She declared that she had an income of $25 per month, and was administratrix of an estate which she would share with her dear sister, if Mary would take her to her home in Oswego. "Only come at once and protect us; let no one know you are here."[13]

Mary could scarcely ignore such a threat to womanhood, though four words in her hand on the wrapper, "Owns two marble mines," suggest an additional inducement. Perhaps the economic motive sped her on her way just a bit faster. She found the princess in need of medical attention, and in no condition to travel. But she nursed her and, eluding the villains, brought her and her companion, also ailing, to Oswego. They settled down in Mary's home but within a few weeks were quarreling over the arrangements. Shortly thereafter the princess and Miss Rheims forsook the farm and found lodging with a neighbor. From this vantage point the princess swore out a warrant against Mary, charging her with third-degree assault. Not to be outdone, the contentious Mary threatened to set upon any official who dared to serve it. The case appears to have ended here, the warrant unserved.

As the year slipped by, Mary became more and more eccentric. She exalted her virtues and assumed an air of infallibility. She was often officious and intolerant, even to friends and relatives. She believed that people were deliberately trying to thwart her and, at times, that her life was in peril.

Perhaps Mary's least excusable foray into public affairs in the name of justice was her intervention in the Almy murder case. On July 16, 1891, a young woman from Concord, New Hampshire, Christie Warden, was brutally murdered. The public was outraged, and a reward of $5000 was offered for the apprehension of the murderer. Frank C. Almy was subsequently arrested, convicted, and hanged.

Meanwhile, Mary had a hired man, one Arthur D. Snoad. She had brought him from New England, and lodged and fed him in her home. Typical of her employees, he remained only a few months before moving on. He subsequently settled in Syracuse. Stirred by the enormity of the Warden homicide, and possibly influenced by the liberal reward, Mary reflected upon the case and came to the startling conclusion that Snoad was the murderer and that New Hampshire had convicted the wrong man.

It is difficult to follow Mary's reasoning in the matter. To the usual processes of deduction she added a reliance upon dreams and spiritualism, a cult which had enjoyed a widespread vogue during her youth. She recalled that Snoad had been missing from the farm at the time of the crime, and that he had returned a few days later exhausted and obviously distressed. She diagnosed blotches on his skin to be a rash caused by water, and concluded that he had swum the Merrimack River at Concord to escape apprehension. She remembered too that some weeks earlier he had spoken affectionately of a girl named Christie, though he had not divulged her surname. She recalled, also, a dream in which she had conversed with Christie Warden. The girl had pointed a finger of accusation at Snoad, and declared that he was her murderer.

Mary also had a theory regarding Frank Almy. She believed that the convicted man, reputed to be Almy, was in reality some one else. The real Almy, alias Henry L. Norcross, she insisted, had been killed a short time earlier, when a bomb which he hurled at the railroad tycoon, Russell Sage, had burst prematurely. To avert a tragic error, Mary plunged into the case with utter abandonment, bordering on the irrational.

She first wrote of her revelations to the Warden family and the local authorities at Concord, but receiving no answer concluded that they plotted a miscarriage of justice in order to collect the reward money. Undaunted, she next set out for New Hampshire to attend to the matter in person. Ten weeks had now elapsed since the date of the crime.

The account of her sleuthing at Concord would read like a comic opera had Mary not been deadly serious. She began her investigation at the Warden home. Believing that she would receive a cool reception, she disguised herself by covering her male habiliments with a long cape. She gained admission and insisted upon remaining overnight on a couch in the living room. Her bizarre appearance and her unusual request, of course, made the Wardens suspicious. Some time after Mary had retired, the father and uncle of the late Christie burst into the room and seized her cloak, presumably to discover her identity. Mary resisted. If her subsequent account of the incident is trustworthy, the altercation was violent. She declared that her nose was fractured in two places and that it bled profusely; also that a dental plate holding two teeth was broken. Her screams aroused other members of the household, who rushed into the room. As they gazed upon the panting victim, Mary remembered that one of the girls had said, "She is making believe."

Having discovered her disguise, the Wardens called the police, who escorted Mary to jail. They held her there for identification for three days, and then offered to release her provided she would pay $8.33 in costs, and promise to leave the state at once. With no alternative except confinement, she paid this sum and departed, after first directing a verbal blast at the Concord constabulary.[14]

But it was not a defeat, only a withdrawal. She continued to tell her story, but apparently found few believers. Just prior to the date for the hanging of the prisoner, she dashed back to New

Hampshire, hoping to stay the execution and obtain a re-investigation. But the trains ran late and, when she arrived in Concord, the trap had already been sprung. She could do nothing more than track down a reporter and spill her story to the press.

The incident served to make her news-worthy, and she capitalized on it to obtain a few speaking engagements in New Hampshire and Massachusetts.

A somewhat different version of Mary's absorption in the Almy case has been told by the daughter of the defense attorney, who was eight years old at the time. She recalls Mary's surprise visit to their home in Plymouth—her trousers, frock coat, and silk hat; also her iron-gray hair cut nearly as short as a man's.

Finding that the attorney was suffering from a nervous breakdown after the exhausting trial—hawkers had reaped a handsome profit selling a cheap edition of the sensational case from door to door—Mary sought the assistance of his wife in what she purported was a campaign to outlaw capital punishment. She declared that there were irregularities in the hanging of Almy. The rope had been too long, and his neck had not broken when the trap was sprung, and the spectators were then ordered to leave the room, and no one really knew what happened thereafter.

Mary's appeal did not move her hostess, and she went off to wage her own battle against capital punishment.[15]

The report that Almy might have escaped the gallows by the king-sized rope was unfounded, but the unconfirmed rumors undoubtedly helped to swell the turnout at Mary's lectures.

Returning to her native soil, Mary repeated her tale of a miscarriage of justice, and of Snoad's guilt to the police at Syracuse. The Oswego press dubbed her charges "the idle vaporing of a crank," and declared that she lived for but one thing, notoriety, but the authorities listened and, after hearing Snoad's defense, held him for further investigation. They did not indict him, however, and he was subsequently released.

The bewildered Snoad then turned the tables on his accuser, by suing Mary for the sum of $10,000 for slander. The trial came before the circuit court at Syracuse in February of 1894, Mary acting as her own counselor. Aware that there were rumors that she was insane, she electrified the overflowing crowd which had packed into the courtroom by proposing that she and Snoad be examined by a commission to determine the lunacy or sanity of each. The offer was refused.

In the course of the testimony Mary managed to elicit a full recital of her experiences. When she spoke of seeing ghosts standing over Snoad's bed, the judge jumped to the attack. "Do you believe in ghosts?" he asked. Without hesitation, Mary shot back, "Do you believe that Christ came back?" The startled judge could find no retort. He had hit a snag!

At this point the judge recessed the court until the following morning and, in the words of the *Syracuse Standard*, "Dr. Mary's cape overcoat, umbrella, badly ruffled silk hat and her tissue-wrapped bundle of 'legal papers' went out into the snow, while Snoad probably wondered whether the circus was worth the price of admission."

At the conclusion of the trial the jury awarded the nominal sum of six cents to Snoad. It had cost her little more than her pride, but other costs were less trivial. The Vanderbilt Hotel, where she had lodged during the trial, would not release her baggage until she paid her bill of $18. The account of the incident closed with Mary exchanging verbal blasts with the adamant manager.[16]

Even less flattering than the Almy episode was Mary's arbitrary conduct in handling property matters involving her family.

In her travels she appears to have been a frequent visitor at her father's old homestead in Greenwich, Massachusetts [now covered by the waters of Quabbin Reservoir], where two maiden aunts, Mary and Vashti Walker, resided. Relationships appear to have been quite friendly for many years. Mary sometimes also stopped at Amherst College nearby to view Walker Hall, which she said was named for one of her forefathers. She became something of an institution there. Upon her arrival, students flocked about her to snap photographs and listen to her banter. Once, she dressed down a young man, who, in answer to a query, directed her to a pair of steps. "Not a pair of steps," she admonished, but a "flight of stairs."[17]

She also used the old Walker home as a center for lecture tours of the surrounding communities. But her stock of good will was quickly dissipated upon the death of her Aunt Mary Walker in 1895. Mary hastened to Greenwich to place the surviving Aunt Vashti under her wing. Apparently conscious of the resentment of relatives who lived in the vicinity, she got the notion that they were prepared to remove her at any cost.

A cousin, Henry M. Woods, reported that she would not drink milk at Aunt Vashti's as "'they' were putting arsenic in it." He also observed that she had told a hack driver that masked men were seeking to waylay her. When Woods steeled himself to ask Mary to leave, "We found all of the best silver belonging to the house locked in her grip-sack, she said for safe keeping." "The most charitable construction I can put on the matter," he advised, "is that she is insane and not accountable for words and deeds." He added that he would breathe easier when he learned Mary was safely at home in Oswego. Meanwhile, until they were certain of it, Aunt Vashti would live in his home.[18]

Mary departed, but at an opportune moment returned to Greenwich and began to pack furnishings for shipment. Cousin Woods discovered six of seven boxes were addressed to Mary in Oswego. He resorted to the law to force an entrance.

Meanwhile, Mary contacted nieces and nephews of the deceased living at points distant from Greenwich to obtain copies of the will, and requested that they ask for her appointment as administratrix of the estate. At least two of the cousins refused her request, one noting that it was a well-known fact that the will was in conformity with their Aunt's plans to leave her property to the church. Both urged Mary to forgo any action to contest the will in the courts. But Mary persevered, only to lose her case and the friendship of the Walker family with it.[19]

But she refused to be sidetracked. She charged that the will which had been filed in the Hampshire probate court was a forgery, and the result of a conspiracy of certain residents of Greenwich. She finally appealed to the Supreme Judicial Court for a new trial, and obtained it. The case was heard at Springfield on September 27, 1897. Acting as her own lawyer, Mary spent the entire afternoon arguing her case—but in vain. The court dismissed the petition, and assigned the costs to her.[20]

Needless to say, she also lost the good will of the Massachusetts branch of the Walkers. The estrangement was complete and irrevocable.

Chapter XI

THE WAY THEY REMEMBER HER

It was inevitable that as the veteran reformer advanced in years she would be identified by her eccentricities by a younger generation, which did not remember the Civil War or Mary's stature in the formative years of the Woman's Suffrage Movement. Many accepted her simply as a queer old woman, dressed in ridiculous clothing and the butt of practical jokes and pranks. There are still dozens of tales, many of them doubtless tall ones, which older residents of the area, particularly those who lived along the route from Bunker Hill to Oswego, will recall at the mention of her name. Only a few, illustrative of her personality, can be retold here.

She is remembered, for example, for her parsimoniousness.

In a conversation at the postoffice in Oswego she learned that a clerk in the office was fond of grapes. On her next trip she brought a basket of this succulent fruit from the vines on her farm and presented them to him. He thanked her profusely. She then purchased some stamps, and turned to walk away without paying for them. The clerk called to her, and tactfully asked her whether she had not forgotten something. Discovering that he would have to be more blunt, he reminded her that she had not paid for the stamps. "Oh," replied Mary, "the grapes will take care of that." She serenely went on her way.

A boy who lived a few doors down Bunker Hill Road from the Walker residence had an experience somewhat similar to the postal clerk's. Mary engaged him to pick up the walnuts which dropped from several trees in her yard and to remove the hulls, a dirty and monotonous job. He remembers the eerie sounds of the wind against the windows between the blows of his mallet, while seated at a bench in a back room of the otherwise empty house. When he at last finished, the Doctor presented him with several quarts of the nuts as his compensation. He remembers his disappointment, and his reluctance to repeat the performance the

137

next year. But when she asked him, he did not refuse.

Other tales illustrate her zeal to accept hospitality where it was not offered. Local Oswego suffragettes, who operated a booth at the New York State Fair at Syracuse just prior to World War I, recall that Mary approached their display, uninvited, straddled the railing—despite her more than eighty years—and helped to dispense the circulars, much to the embarrassment of all others concerned. The crowd swelled.

A somewhat similar situation developed one day at the home of an acquaintance in Oswego. The little doctor dropped in, tired and dry, after her long walk from Bunker Hill, and asked for a glass of milk, her favorite beverage. When her hostess complied, Mary offered her thanks, but remarked that it was too much; and then, without waiting for a response, she continued, "It won't go to waste, I'll finish it in the morning." Again, before the startled hostess could muster a reply to her uninvited guest, Mary added, "Don't bother to make up a bed; I'll sleep with Florence [the daughter]." Without pausing for an answer, the dapper visitor hurried up the stairs to see that the bed was ready for her and Florence.

On the other hand, Mary is occasionally remembered as being more generous. In her walks to and from her home and Furniss Station, the nearest railroad depot, she sometimes stopped at a home about midway between the two for lunch. She came without notification, but after she had gone her host always found a coin under Mary's plate.

There are also stories relating the practical jokes perpetrated upon the old woman, at a safe distance of course, to observe her proverbial anger.

One day she drove into town in her ancient buggy, propelled by an almost equally venerable horse. She tied up at the county building, and went inside to transact her business. Her arrival was not unobserved by a gang of teen-aged boys who were lounging in the park. They quickly went into action. While one watched lest the unpredictable doctor return at once to her horse and rig, the others unhitched Dolly (or perhaps it was Molly), and turned her around, and hitched her again with her head facing the buggy. They then crossed the street to a safe observation point behind the library to watch Mary's reaction. When she saw her predicament, she shouted her displeasure and shook her fist (or umbrella) at her unseen assailants who, of course, were convulsed with laughter.

Another, featuring her horse and buggy, involved a hitching contest at a farmers' picnic at Oswego Beach. Mary took pride in her facility with harness, probably for the same reason that she liked to think that she could dress faster than a man, and entered the competition. On signal, contestants backed their horses between the shafts, threw the harness over the horse, and began to work with the buckles. The first to complete the hitching won the prize. On this occasion Mary became so engrossed in the harness that she did not see a boy, who had sneaked to the opposite side of her horse, unhook the harness as fast as she could fasten it. It was great fun for the spectators, several of whom never forgot it.

A final horse story relates a prank involving several Bunker Hill boys. One evening they went quietly into Mary's barn, placed the harness on her horse as it munched grain in the stall. They next mixed up a batch of heavy soap suds and coated the unsuspecting horse with it. Then they removed the harness carefully, so as to leave its imprint contrasting sharply with the hardening lather. The next morning they made an early appearance on a neighbor's porch across the road. They saw Mary enter the stable, then emerge quickly, muttering as she hastened to summon help. "Some one took Fred out last night," she exploded, "and drove him unmercifully. I am afraid he is going to collapse." Only after one of her adult neighbors examined the off-color Fred more closely was the hoax revealed.

Other tales relate to situations arising from Mary's male attire:

One time when Mary was residing in a Syracuse hotel, and suffering from a lame leg, she called on the Irish maid to help her dress. The embarrassed girl ran to the manager, and told him of the request. "Go ahead, and help," he ordered. Shaking her head with obvious disbelief, she responded, "Sure Oi niver saw the loikes o' that afore."[1]

There is a yarn too about her pants with a bit of international flavor:

The Chinese Minister to the United States, Wu Ting-fang, asked Mary why she wore pants.

"Why do you wear a skirt?" she parried.

"It is the custom of my country," the dignified Wu answered.

'It is the custom in *my* country to do as one pleases," quipped the irrepressible Mary.

139

Fred Barnes, for many years a furrier in Oswego, told the following story about the fur jacket which Mary wore over her Prince Albert coat during the winter months:

"The village wags used to say that every one knew that Noah took two minks into the Ark with him, but that nobody knew what become of one of them. The other was in Dr. Mary's cape."

The most frequently repeated story relating to her clothing was that she was the only woman ever authorized to wear pants by the Congress of the United States. The claim was made in her obituaries, and is accepted as fact by the residents of the Oswego area. One woman recalls that her father, a former Chief of Police in Oswego, interceded to obtain such an authorization to protect Mary from mob violence and arrest by unenlightened police.

But Mary, of course, would have been the last to seek such permission from anyone, including the all-male Congress, for what she believed was a natural right. She commented upon the rumor in 1912, while testifying before a Congressional committee. She attributed it to a statement which appeared in a Washington newspaper and in the *New York Herald* under a picture of her. She called it amusing, but declared that she wished to scotch the myth, now and forever. Apparently, few read her denial; and the story endures.

There are also many anecdotes relating to her extreme egotism. One is that on a Fourth of July in Oswego as she walked toward festivities in the park, she passed in front of a low-hanging flag. She stopped, turned to a cluster of children gawking at her, and then kissed the flag. "There," she exclaimed, "you'll never forget that you saw Dr. Mary Walker kiss Old Glory."

There is also the tale of the individual who dared to talk back to the imperious doctor, and lived to get the best of her:

Mary entered the Delaware, Lackawanna and Western station in Oswego one morning, and accosted the young call man, who was quietly smoking. "Sir, if you would read the scientific works I have read, you would know that nicotine of tobacco which you are inhaling is deleterious to your system. You are committing suicide, and have no business to pollute the air." When she paused, the young man replied gently, "You seem a stranger to scientific works I have read. They have taught me one important lesson." "What is that," asked Mary. "They teach me to mind my own business."

Though set back for a moment, Mary refused to drop the subject. "Come now, why do you make a fool of yourself in destroying your health?" "I'll answer you," he responded, "if you will first answer my question." "Agreed," said the little lady. "Why do you make a d——d fool of yourself by parading around in men's breeches?"

The Doctor, for once speechless, was seen soon thereafter, like Don Quixote, behind her Rosinante, making the best possible time for Bunker Hill.[4]

An Oswego physician recalls a series of incidents involving Dr. Mary with three generations of his family.[5] When a boy, his mother told him of her experiences as a student of Mary's at the village school in Minetto. Later, in the 1890s, he remembers that upon his arrival in Brooklyn to attend medical college, a fellow student, learning that he came from Oswego, remarked, "Why you are from the place with the old fort [Fort Ontario] and that woman doctor who wears pants." A few years after entering the medical profession in Oswego, he answered a knock at the door one evening to find Dr. Mary awaiting him. He invited her to come inside, and a moment later overheard his five-year-old son inquire in a stage whisper from his perch on the railing of the stairway, "Who is the woman?" Receiving no answer, the child presumably glanced down the steps to see for himself. His second query followed immediately: "I mean, who is the man?"

It turned out that Dr. Mary had called to attend a meeting of the Oswego Medical Academy which was scheduled at the physician's home that evening. Her presence was unexpected since the medics studiously ignored her. Mary seems to have had a mission in mind; perhaps it was to seek help for her campaign against compulsory vaccination for smallpox, which she was waging at this time. As the members of the Academy arrived, as though by signal, they lit their pipes or cigars, and began to puff with gusto. The room was soon blue with smoke. It was more than Mary could bear. Without waiting for the formal opening of the business, she edged to the door, and made her escape from the poisonous atmosphere, her mission unaccomplished.

An anecdote published in one of Mary's obituaries illustrates the manner in which myths took root and flourished, and in turn, were accepted as truth. In November, 1895, while she was in Massachusetts looking after her interests in the estate of her

141

deceased Aunt Mary Walker, a certain Miss M. J. Smith debarked from the steamship *Germanic* at New York. She wore male attire, and was mistaken for Dr. Mary Walker traveling incognito. The *New York Evening World* reported:

> Dr. Mary Walker was ill in her cabin most of the time during the tempestuous voyage of the *Germanic,* which arrived this morning. Dr. Mary is not a good sailor, and if she has been called strong minded, the *Germanic's* stewardesses can bear testimony to her weakness in other respects. On the ship's passenger list Dr. Walker appeared simply as Miss M. J. Smith. An up-to-date young man wearing long hair and a big chrysanthemum met Dr. Walker and her friend, Miss Schenck, and whisked them off to No. 312 West Fourteenth Street.

Within several days the account was repeated in newspapers in Philadelphia, Buffalo, and points west.

The *Oswego Palladium* at once exposed the error to local readers, pointing out that she was in Massachusetts, and that "Miss M. J. Smith must be a counterfeit. Beware of her." But the story did not die; it grew.

Twenty-four years later, it had been embellished to include a presentation to Queen Victoria; a gift from the Queen of a gold watch and chain, which Mary had cherished to the end of her life. The crossing of the Atlantic by the *Germanic,* it was said, had been the roughest in history. Research confirms only the last of these observations. The Atlantic was unusually roiled in November of 1895, but Mary did not see or feel it. She was busily obstructing the plans of her Massachusetts relatives for a quiet and peaceful disposition of Aunt Mary Walker's property.

Not as well remembered as her eccentricities by younger contemporaries was Mary's occasional tenderness. When her Mother died in 1886 after a long illness, she hurried home from Washington to arrive just before the funeral. A few days later she wrote an open letter in the local paper expressing her "delicate appreciation" to the Rev. Dr. Tully and the Rev. Mr. Corbin "for beautifully and tenderly officiating at the funeral of my Mother in the School building on a part of hers and my father's homestead estate that they gave to the district as a site for the same."[7]

Chapter XII

LAST CRUSADES

Mary never retired from the strenuous pace of her activities; age simply slowed down the momentum. She spent more time on her farm now, sometimes with a housekeeper, sometimes alone. Occasionally, also, acquaintances, whom she had met on her travels, came for short or more extended visits, some expecting to receive medical care. A former neighbor recalls that she sometimes locked these guests in the house when she went off to town, and remembers that one such victim shouted and pounded until she attracted passers-by, who secured help from local residents to force the door and free the hapless woman.

Another time, Mary's guest was a clairvoyant, whom she induced to give a demonstration for the neighbors. A witness recalls that the artist would perform only when there was appropriate music, and that his mother filled the void with their gramophone and cylindrical records. When the music began she appeared to go into a trance and, while so engaged, described events which she could not have known from experience: for example, the death of his brother, which had occurred several years before. She varied her performance by painting a mysterious and presumably formless scene to the accompaniment of music. She then turned it a half-circle to reveal an exquisite landscape. The evening was a huge success.

When not engaged elsewhere she tended her garden, and occasionally delivered the surplus in town. A few residents recall purchasing her vegetables and berries. One of these was the ladies' tailor, who made her coat and pants. More than a half-century later he recalls that she was always pleasant, and paid for her clothes promptly.

Elderly residents of Oswego remember the frequent trips in her creaking old buggy, and a few recall that she invited them to take a seat in the vehicle and drove them into town. In her last years, as both she and the horse and buggy wore out, they saw

143

her ride to town with an accommodating neighbor.

A local resident of Scriba recalls that while returning from a trip to Oswego he saw Mary stepping gingerly along the muddy road. He stopped and offered her a ride, which she eagerly accepted. She was courteous and friendly and, when he came to the fork of the road where he ordinarily turned toward his home, he went on, knowing that the doctor would be en route to the home of her sister, Luna Griswold. When they arrived at the Griswolds, the old physician stepped lightly to the ground, and lifted her straw hat [it was summer] as she returned her thanks for the ride.

To all appearances Mary was now absorbed in the quiet life of the neighborhood, but she was always ready to drop the mundane, when duty called in Washington or Albany. In 1897 in the armory over the old Central Market in Washington, she addressed the first Congress of Mothers, an audience of two thousand, which was later to become the National Congress of Parents and Teachers.[1] Occasionally, she lobbied for widows' pensions and woman's suffrage in her old haunts. She also made almost annual pilgrimages to Albany to testify on suffrage and other matters which caught her fancy. In 1911, for example, she appeared as a witness in support of the McManus-Boylan bill, designed to permit the admission of children to school whose parents conscientiously opposed vaccination. Testifying before the Health Committee of the Senate and Assembly she insisted that claims for vaccination as a preventive for smallpox were grossly exaggerated, and that much of it was done for the fees involved. She recommended onions as a deterrent, declaring that she had once advised the King of Spain on their use to combat an epidemic of smallpox in Madrid. Later, she continued, the Spanish newspapers had hailed her as "The Great American Life Saver."[2]

A year after her assault upon vaccination she was back in Albany to argue against the Brackett Equal Suffrage bill, objecting to its techniques, not the purpose of the bill. Again, in 1915, she was at the State Capitol as a witness before the Suffrage Committee of the New York State Constitutional Convention. Her testimony indicated that her approach to suffrage had not varied during half a century.

On a trip to New York in 1912 she was stricken with pneu-

144

monia, but she recovered sufficiently to return to Oswego a few weeks later.

Speaking engagements came less frequently now, but in 1912 she undertook what the newspapers identified as a tour of western New York. To her stock-in-trade she added a lecture on "A Safe and Sane Fourth of July," which included a protest against the usual slaughter from fireworks, and an analysis of the basic meaning of the holiday.

Despite the fact that she was increasingly out of touch with new medical science, she did not hesitate to speak out on professional matters. In 1910 she pronounced as "humbug" the theory that germs caused tuberculosis. "No microbes or germs can live in the live tissues of the lungs," she declared. "They are not the cause of tubercules, but the result of worn-out tissue. Tubercules are formed by smoke, and tobacco smoke is worse than any other kind because the cinders are more poisonous, containing nicotine." She had not retreated an iota from her earlier diagnosis of the evils of tobacco.[3]

Having set aright the causes of tuberculosis, she next indicated that she had discovered a way to prevent heart failure brought on by overwork, mental strain or spasmodic coughing. When there was an unusual palpitation of the heart, she advised that the left hand be placed just below the heart with the fingers pointing to the center of the chest. The right hand should then be placed over the left, with the fingers touching the left wrist, and pressure applied upon the heart until it began to beat normally. This would control circulation but would not stop it, as the ribs prevented pressure which would be injurious. She predicted that her discovery would save many lives![4]

She also had some words of advice for Czar Nicholas II of Russia, who was blessed with four daughters, but no son. The Czar consulted with fortune tellers, mystics and charlatans in his quest for an heir, and Mary, aware of his plight, sent him her diagnosis of his difficulties. Unfortunately, she does not seem to have kept a copy of it; nor is there evidence that Nicholas received it or acted upon it. In any event, Mary was elated when the Tsarevitch was born and was willing to accept some of the credit for it. She added the story to her repertory. An Oswegonian, who visited her home in the summer of 1911 remembers the story from Mary's lips, and recalls the lifting of eyebrows which accompanied her discussion of this delicate subject.[5]

During these years Mary became more and more concerned with her place in history. She arranged the furnishings of her home to give it the appearance of a museum, featuring herself. She displayed her pictures, diplomas, clippings and scrapbooks, and a variety of curios which she had received at conventions and on the lecture circuit. She also set out antiques to show the modern generation the handicrafts of the pioneers, items which she apparently gathered from the Walker homestead and the furnishings of her late aunts in Massachusetts. Of particular interest was the chair which she said had once graced the White House; and not to be overlooked, a portrait of her mother painted by an unknown itinerant, and another of herself, sketched upon the paneling in the hallway. A conspicuous and oft enforced "No Smoking" sign added Mary's inimitable touch to the scene.

In July, 1891, a group of young ladies, who were taking courses at the Oswego Normal School, walked out to Bunker Hill to visit the famous reformer, their ankle-long skirts stirring the dusty road. They at length arrived at the neat white cottage and entered the gate, which was flanked by a picket fence. From the barn in the rear they heard an unmistakably feminine voice directing the transfer of hay from a wagon to the mow. In a few moments they saw a small figure, clad in long pants, a knee-length coat, and a man's straw hat, emerge from the barn. There was nothing masculine, however, about the gait, which was ladylike. It, of course, was Dr. Mary. She invited them to take chairs on the lawn while she finished her chore at the barn, and observing the jaded appearance of her guests, added with a bit of sarcasm that they would not be tired if they were not dressed in such obsolete gowns.

After a lengthy wait the front door opened, and Dr. Mary, now dressed in a linen duster, appeared. Her iron gray hair was combed back, and fell loosely to her collar. She invited them to inspect the house, and led them from room to room. She was cordial, but took her responsibility seriously, and assumed that her visitors were interested in the details of her life. She showed them a burled maple rope bed in which she was born, and other old Walker furnishings. From a closet in the attic she extracted a hoop-skirt and a pair of corsets, which she termed "relics of barbarism." She then exhibited a photograph of herself in a Prince

Albert coat and pants, as she appeared, she declared, when attending social functions at Washington. In the recital of her experiences in the Civil War she took time to berate General Grant. It would appear that his long illness and heroic last hours failed to mollify her.

When she discovered that her guests were teachers, she told them of her experiences as a teacher forty years before; that she started at $1 per week, and boarded around. Several weeks later she saw several of the young women as she drove by the campus. She stopped and told them that she now recalled that she had received up to $3 a week for her services as a teacher.[6]

Another young visitor recalls a similar tour of Mary's house some twenty years after the one mentioned above. An added feature was an American flag stretched across the maple bed in which she was born.

Mary's rendezvous with destiny is obvious, also, in a picture which she had taken to show how she would appear in her coffin. It reveals her in the usual posture, eyes closed, and clad in her finest masculine regalia with a flag across her breast!

In keeping with the high evaluation which she placed upon her career was her offer of her home as a museum to the New York Historical Association.

Preliminaries to the proposal began in October, 1913, when the association held its annual convention at Oswego. The theme of the meeting was the military tradition of the old forts there, and one of the papers was presented by the young and handsome Assistant Secretary of the Navy, Franklin Delano Roosevelt. The sessions terminated with a parade to Montcalm Park, where a commemorative plaque was unveiled. As officials and distinguished guests awaited the start of the parade on the porch of the Pontiac Hotel, the diminutive, eighty-one-year-old Mary· pushed her way through the crowd. The local Congressman, Luther Mott, welcomed her, and introduced her to the guests. Mary at once singled out F.D.R., to whom she volunteered her misgivings about the other Roosevelt. She added the reassurance, however, that he appeared to be a different kind of person. In the midst of her discourse on the relations of the United States with revolutionary Mexico, the parade started, and a gallant marshal whisked her into an empty seat in the motor cavalcade. An alert photographer preserved the sight, a touring car with the top down, and Mary, head covered with her high silk hat, seated between two of the guests.[7]

The Association's dedication to history made a deep impression upon Mary, and two years later she offered her house to that body, provided it would be preserved as a shrine. The Board of Trustees appointed a committee of one, Dr. James Riggs, Principal of the Oswego Normal School, to investigate and report. At a subsequent meeting of the Board he recommended that the proposal be declined; and so it was.[8]

Mary was more successful in her bid for membership in the Daughters of the American Revolution, though it required perseverance, and a final tactical maneuver to storm the ramparts. There was no question regarding her eligibility. Her great-grandfather, Jesse Snow, had fought in both the American Revolution and the French and Indian War. Nevertheless, her application for membership was refused. According to an unidentified clipping in the Walker papers, the board decided that the society, being composed of women, could not consider this candidate eligible or acceptable, since she had repudiated the recognized apparel of women. This version of her rejection would appear to be inaccurate, however, since admittance requires an approval of the candidate's personal qualifications by the local chapter, approval which the Oswego chapter would not grant. Mary did not yield; she simply shifted her ground, applying for membership elsewhere. She finally gained her objective in 1914 with an election to full membership in the Cornelia Greene Chapter in St. Louis, Missouri, lineage number 108,250. Records show that she never attended a meeting of the chapter, but she added her membership to her printed list of qualifications as a lecturer.[9]

Mary's final bid for the spotlight elicited a column in the press, and might have produced headlines if her long-shot gamble had succeeded. Five days after Congress declared war on Germany in April, 1917, she dispatched a cablegram from Washington to the German Kaiser, calling upon him to stop the war, and to hold a peace conference at her farm on Bunker Hill.

Addressing the Emperor as "His Royal Highness," she declared that he was the only living person with "such a wonderful eminence in military affairs," that he could order a cease-fire. As soon as he had taken this action, she was prepared to invite him, and such others as he might choose, to her home for a general peace

148

conference. Her offer was unqualified, except that she would not permit the consumption of intoxicants. Though she did not ordinarily allow smoking, she would make an exception for confirmed users. She would make available to the participants stenographers, typewriters, and telephone, a daily mail delivery, and an ample menu. She would also arrange automobile transportation from Oswego, and a train escort from New York, all without cost.

As inducements for his acceptance, she held out the flattering prospect of world-wide recognition. "By your act here in this peace measure, I see that down the declivity of time your Royal Highness will be considered the greatest in war, and what is a thousandfold more important, the greatest in peace measures, and the leader in doing away with armaments." A huge monument would be raised on Bunker Hill in his honor, and others in every country in the world.

If it met with his approval, she would invite the President of the United States, the Secretary of State, and the Speaker of the House of Representatives, and their wives. And because of the immediacy of the project, she proposed that the conference begin as early as May or June; and to facilitate her arrangements, she requested that he inform her as to the size of his delegation.

To add status to her novel proposal, she reminded the Kaiser that she had been a surgeon in the American Civil War, and had received the Medal of Honor.[10]

There appears to have been no reply from his Royal Highness, but it goes without saying that he received worse advice! The Oswego press carried the cablegram in full, but could not resist a bit of editorializing in the headline: "No Information as to Who Pays for the Cable." It offered no other editorial comment. History might add that it was a lost opportunity for the Kaiser, and possibly for the world!

Several developments in the last months of Mary's life undoubtedly gave her deep satisfaction. With our entrance into World War I women flocked into the factories for war jobs. There was no place there for the frills of the feminine wardrobe. Overnight, it seemed, the American woman lifted the hemline of her skirts, or abandoned them for trousers. For sixty years Mary had been doing a solo performance in pants; now she had thousands of confederates.

An article released by the United Press under the caption: "Have You Your Trouserettes?" graphically indicated their popularity. After first giving credit to Mary for blazing the trail for the masculine nether garments, it pointed out that a whimsy of fate, that is, the war, made pants a blessing in disguise for not only the advanced female but also housewives and mothers. The pants habit had become so fascinating, it observed, that the 1917 female could not even doff them at night, and that after the window shades were drawn "she dons cute little suits of pajamas with feminine V-cut décolleté and short-sleeved uppers and masculine straight-cut, ankle-length lowers.

"So you see, it keeps lovely women *panting* twenty-four hours a day to keep up with these strenuous times."[11]

Mary was no longer alone!

A second sweeping change, sped toward consummation by the war, was Prohibition. Mary was not a professional temperance crusader; she never abandoned the Democratic for the Prohibition Party. But she had preached temperance for more than a half-century. Now the end of the evil of alcohol was in sight; or, at least, so it seemed!

A final dramatic and challenging reform was woman's suffrage. The movement had not shaped up as Mary had wished, but the Constitutional Amendment of 1917 granted the privilege to the women of New York, and the Nineteenth Amendment to the Federal Constitution would soon make it universal.

A few weeks before drafting her cablegram to Kaiser Wilhelm, Mary fell while climbing the steps of the Capitol in Washington. She never completely recovered from the injury, though she was not mortally ill until several months before her death two years later.

One of her last labors was to put her finances in order. She had managed to pay off the mortgage which came with the title to her farm, but had been forced to borrow money from time to time, using the property as security. A nephew, Byron Worden, was particularly helpful; and in return for past favors, and the assumption of costs which might attend her last illness, she deeded her farm to him. Except for the house, the property now had little value. She did not write a will.

During her final sickness she was taken to the General Hospital Number Five at Fort Ontario in Oswego, an almost unprecedented procedure, but in keeping with her whole career. War Department records show that she entered the hospital on August 5, 1918, and that she was discharged some time during September. An old associate of the suffragist trail, Nellie B. Van Slingerland, of New Jersey, learning that Mary was sick and without funds, hastened to Oswego to assist her. She had Mary removed to the home of a neighbor at Bunker Hill, Mrs. Frank Dwyer, where she was tenderly cared for.[12]

In one of her last recorded interviews she recalled her early years, when doors opened to her everywhere. "Presidents and cabinet ministers and great generals were glad to meet and listen to me. I was younger then, and I was working for our soldier boys, just as so many girls and young women are working in the Red Cross for our boys who are over there [in France]." Then, with a touch of pathos, she continued, "But now I am alone with the infirmities of age fast weighing me down and practically penniless, and no one wants to be bothered with me." She would not grovel in self-pity, however, and concluded, "But it is the same experiences that have come to others, and why should I complain?"[13]

Death came to the old warrior on February 21, 1919, at the age of eighty-six.

Newspapers in distant Florida and California hurriedly scanned their files to reprint the colorful tales of her life.

One erroneous report, which had circulated for many years, was now repeated as fact—that she had been the only woman authorized to wear men's clothes by an act of Congress. The story continues forty years after her death.

A simple funeral service was held in the old homestead. Even hymns were omitted, and only the ubiquitous American flag over her casket indicated special recognition. She was buried in her black frock suit in the family plot in Rural Cemetery in Oswego Town, about two miles from her home. Later, a headstone with the inscription, "Mary," was placed over her grave. And twenty years later the Elmina Spencer Tent of the Daughters of Union Veterans accepted responsibility for the care of the plot. The action was appropriate, for Elmina Spencer, a Civil War nurse, was Oswego's second Civil War heroine.

History, despite Mary's sense of it, has not been kind to her. Her early withdrawal from the leadership of the Woman's Suffrage Movement dulled her luster as a suffragist, and the public's absorption in two World Wars dimmed interest in the Great War, for a time, at least, until the approach of its centennial. Even her acquaintances at the time of her death knew little of her early achievements, and remembered her only for her eccentricities and her egotism.

With no children, and no immediate relatives to bear the Walker name, her brother having preceded her to the grave, and no moneyed foundation to perpetuate her name, Mary soon dropped out of sight. The homestead burned a few years after her death, and only the broken foundation stones remain visible today. Fortunately, some of her effects, including her medals, some papers and books, and a portrait of her mother, had been taken to the home of a nephew, and were not lost.

Nevertheless, she keeps popping up when least expected. She was remembered in New York State's Freedom Train, where documents illustrative of her work for woman's suffrage were displayed. The Congress of Parents and Teachers in 1960 recalled her services upon their sixty-third anniversary, and a portrait of Mary in her Civil War uniform was recently discovered in the old Army Medical Museum in Washington. Now the centennial of the Civil War will inevitably rediscover her—in a Washington Hospital, on her way to the western front, a prisoner in Castle Thunder, or in a Matthew Brady photograph in her petite surgeon's costume.

Notes to Chapter I

1. The diary is in the possession of Mrs. Charles Sivers, Oswego, N. Y.
2. J. B. R. Walker, *Memorial of the Walkers of the Old Plymouth Colony,* Northampton, Mass., 1861. Newspaper clipping in volume in Sivers mss.
3. *Oswego Times,* February 22, 1919.
4. Advertisement in *Hit* by Dr. Mary E. Walker, New York, 1871.
5. Fred P. Wright, "Dr. Mary E. Walker," *Yearbook,* Oswego County Historical Society, 1953, pp. 46-53.
6. Among books in the Sivers mss.
7. J. E. Gifford to Mary Walker, September 2, 1855, Sivers mss.
8. Poynter mss. Woman's Medical College of Pennsylvania.
9. *Ibid.*
10. Walker mss., Syracuse University, affidavit of L. J. Worden at Utica, March 21, 1866.
11. Sivers mss.
12. *Rome Sentinel,* March 14, 1860.

Notes to Chapter II

1. *Sibyl,* I, No. 20, Middletown, N. Y., April 15, 1857.
2. *Ibid.,* II, No. 21, May 1, 1858.
3. *Ibid.,* II, No. 1, July 1, 1857.
4. *Ibid.,* III, No. 2, July 15, 1858.
5. *Ibid.,* III, No. 22, May 15, 1859.
6. *Ibid.,* III, No. 16, February 15, 1859.
7. *Ibid.,* IV, No. 3, August 1, 1859; IV, No. 6, September 15, 1859.
8. *Ibid.,* III, No. 16, February 15, 1859.
9. *Dubuque* (Iowa) *Herald,* May 27, 1869.
10. *History of Delaware County, Iowa,* Chicago, 1878.
11. July 12, 1865. Walker mss., Syracuse University.
12. March 27, 1866. Walker mss., Oswego County Historical Society.
13. Walker mss., Syracuse University.

Notes to Chapter III

1. Walker mss., Oswego County Historical Society.
2. "Notes Connected with the Army," Walker mss., Syracuse University.
3. *Ibid.*
4. *Ibid.*
5. "Notes Connected with the Army," cited by Mrs. Eric Lawson, "Dr. Mary Walker," unpublished master's thesis, Syracuse University, pp. 17-18. See also George W. Adams, *Doctors in Blue,* New York, 1952, p. 176.

6. "Notes Conunected with the Army."
7. *Ibid.*
8. Poynter mss.
9. *Sibyl,* VI, No. 7, October 1, 1861.
10. Walker mss., Syracuse University.
11. "Notes Connected with the Army."
12. *Ibid.* See also *Oswego Times,* November 26, December 1, 5, 1862.
13. "Notes Connected with the Army."
14. *Ibid.* See also Adams, *op. cit.,* Chapter VI.
15. *Sibyl,* VII, No. 9, November 1, 1862.
16. *Ibid.* VII, No. 8, October 15, 1862.
17. *Ibid.* VIII, No. 1, July 1, 1863.
18. *Oswego Times,* May 9, 1863.
19. *New York Tribune,* quoted in *Oswego Times,* June 19, 1863.
20. *Oswego Times,* March 24, 1863.

Notes to Chapter IV

1. Quoted in Helen B. Woodward, *The Bold Women,* New York: Farrer, Straus & Cudahy, Inc. 1953, p. 292. Used by permission. The unfavorable report was commented upon, also, by a member of the army board in the *New York Medical Journal,* V (1867), No. 2, 167-170.
2. *London Evening Star,* April 6, 1867, in Sivers mss.
3. Woodward, *op. cit.,* pp. 289-290.
4. *Leicester Journal,* April 5, 1867, in Sivers mss.
5. Poynter mss.
6. "Notes Connected with the Army."
7. *Ibid.*
8. Sivers mss., in an undated clipping.
9. August 25, 1864.
10. Sivers mss., in an undated clipping.
11. *Ibid.*
12. *Richmond Examiner,* May 13, 1864.
13. *Newcastle Daily Chronicle* (England), March 26, 1867, in Sivers mss.
14. Sivers mss.
15. *Ibid.*
16. *Oswego Times,* September 15, 1864.
17. *Ibid.* October 25, 1864; December 24, 1864.
18. Sivers mss.
19. Copy in Poynter mss.
20. Archives, Department of Defense, E. T. Conley to Francis D. Culkin, March 2, 1937, quoted by Fred P. Wright, *loc. cit.*
21. *Ibid.*
22. Sivers mss.
23. *Ibid,* in an unidentified newspaper clipping.
24. *Congressional Record,* Senate Report 602, 50th Congress, 1st Session, 30; quoted by Lawson, *op. cit.*

25. William H. Edsell, July —, 1873, copy in Walker mss., Syracuse University.

26. April —, 1865, copy in Poynter mss.

27. April 22, 1865.

28. Original in Walker mss., Oswego County Historical Society.

29. More than 1,000 awards of the Congressional Medal of Honor were rescinded after the Civil War in an effort to increase the prestige of the grant.

Notes to Chapter V

1. *Washington Daily Chronicle*, May 25, 1872.

2. Walker mss., Oswego County Historical Society.

3. Dr. Hasbrouck to Dr. Mary Walker, July 27, 1865, Poynter mss.

4. *New York Evening Express*, June 14, 1866. See also *New York Sun*, June 14, 1866, and the *New York Times*, June 6, 1866.

5. Sivers mss., an unidentified clipping.

6. *New York Times*, June 6, 1866; *New York World*, June 14, 1866.

7. Sivers mss., an unidentified clipping.

Notes to Chapter VI

1. Sivers mss.

2. *Glasgow Herald*, October 12, 1866.

3. *Manchester Guardian*, October 10, 1866; *Glasgow Herald*, October 12, 1866; *Manchester Courier*, October 10, 1866.

4. *Glasgow Herald*, October 12, 1866.

5. Walker mss., Syracuse University.

6. *Ibid.*

7. *London Daily News*, November 21, 1866. See also *London Morning Star*, November 21, 1866: *Franco-American* (n.d.), Sivers mss.; *London Morning Post*, November 21, 1866.

8. *Morning Star*, November 21, 1866; *London Daily News*, November 21, 1866; *Franco-American* (n.d.), Sivers mss.

9. *Morning Advertiser*, November 29, 1866.

10. December 1, 1866.

11. *New York Medical Journal*, IV (January, 1867), No. 22, 314-316.

12. *Medical Press and Circular*, quoted in *New York Medical Journal*, IV (January, 1867), No. 22, 316.

13. Roberts Bartholow, late Assistant Surgeon, U.S. Army, *New York Medical Journal*, V (1867), No. 2, 167-170.

14. *London Morning Star*, February 22, 1867.

15. *West London Observer*, March 9, 1867.

16. A. Courtney to Dr. Mary Walker, April 9, 1867, Walker mss., Oswego County Historical Society.

17. Morison Kyle to G. W. Muir, Walker mss., Syracuse University.

18. Moncure Daniel Conway, *Autobiography*, Boston, 1905, II, 174-175.

19. August 3, 1867.

20. Sivers mss., in an unidentified clipping.
21. *Human Nature, A Monthly Journal of Zoistic Science* (London), September, 1867, in Sivers mss.
22. Walker mss., Syracuse University.

Notes to Chapter VII

1. Sivers mss., clippings.
2. *Fulton Telegraph,* October 22, 1869.
3. *Kansas City Evening Bulletin,* November 11, 1869.
4. *Ibid.* November 19, 1869.
5. Poynter mss.
6. New York, American News Company, 1871.
7. *Hit,* p. 30.
8. *Ibid,* p. 66.
9. *Ibid,* p. 133.
10. *New York World,* February —, 1893, Walker mss., Syracuse University, quoted by Lawson, *op. cit.,* p. 91.
11. *Hit,* pp. 176-177.
12. *Ibid,* p. 177.
13. *Nashua Daily Telegraph* (New Hampshire), November 11, 1893.
14. William H. Boyd, Philadelphia, 1878.
15. Chapter I.

Notes to Chapter VIII

1. *Washington National Republican* (n.d.), Sivers mss.
2. *Washington Morning Chronicle,* April 29, 1869.
3. Walker mss., Syracuse University.
4. *Cincinnati Commercial,* September 17, 1871.
5. *Ibid.*
6. *Washington Daily Chronicle,* February 1, 1871.
7. *New York Sun,* October 10, 1870.
8. *Washington Evening Star,* March 18, 1871.
9. *Ibid.* April 14, 1871.
10. *Washington Sunday Morning Gazette,* April 16, 1871.
11. Elizabeth Cady Stanton, Susan B. Anthony and Matilda Joslyn Gage (eds.), *History of Woman Suffrage,* Rochester, 1887, II, 813.
12. Belva Lockwood to Dr. Mary Walker, July 29, 1871, Walker mss., Syracuse University.
13. *Washington Daily Patriot,* January 25, 1872.
14. *Oswego Palladium,* November 4, 1880. See also unidentified newspaper clipping dated Oswego, February 22, ——, Walker mss., Syracuse University.
15. Unpublished biography of Belva A. Lockwood by Lella Crum Gardner, daughter of Belva Lockwood.

16. *Daily Journal* (Lockport, N. Y.), February 11, 1874.
17. Dr. Mary E. Walker, *Crowning Constitutional Argument*, Oswego, 1907.
18. Ida Husted Harper (ed.), *History of Woman Suffrage*, C. 1922, III, 103.
19. *Crowning Constitutional Argument*.
20. *Ibid*.
21. *Oswego Palladium*, February 22, 1911.
22. Hearings before the Committee on the Judiciary, House of Representatives, No. 1, "Woman Suffrage," by Dr. Mary E. Walker, February 14, 1912, 62nd Congress, 2nd Session, Washington, 1912.
23. Hearings before the Committee on the Judiciary, House of Representatives, Serial 11, Part 2 and 3, "Statement of Dr. Mary E. Walker on Woman Suffrage," pp. 96-99, 64th Congress, 1st Session, Washington, 1916. See also Harper, *op. cit.*, V, 438.
24. Mary E. Walker to Patrick W. Cullinan, May 14, 22, June 6, 16, July —, 1915; Mary E. Walker to Luther Mott, July 14, 1915, New York State Library.
25. Luther Mott to Patrick W. Cullinan, July 16, 1915, New York State Library.
26. Address in Dr. Walker's hand in New York State Library, Archives Division.
27. Mary E. Walker to Patrick W. Cullinan (n.d.), New York State Library.

Notes to Chapter IX

1. *Washington Sunday Gazette*, April, 1871.
2. *Oswego Times*, June 1, 1892.
3. *Ibid.* June 15, 17, 18, 1892.
4. *Oswego Palladium*, October 14, 1896.
5. Copy in Walker mss., Syracuse University.
6. *Syracuse Herald*, September 18, 1901.
7. *Oswego Palladium Times*, February 5, 1941.
8. *Oswego Palladium*, April 16, 1904.
9. *Oswego Times*, June 30, 1904.
10. May 25, 1872.
11. *Chicago Herald*, December 13, 1880; *Utica Saturday Globe*, December 27, 1890.
12. *Chicago Herald*, December 13, 1880, quoted by Lawson, *op. cit.*, pp. 56-57.
13. *Congressional Record*, 55th Congress, 2nd Session, H.R. 9732.
14. *Ibid.* 45th Congress, 1st Session, H.R. 896; House Miscellaneous Documents, 45th Congress, V, 1877-1878.
15. Ben. Perley Poore, *Reminiscences*, Philadelphia, 1886, II, 457-458.
16. Walker mss., National Archives.
17. *Ibid*.
18. *Ibid*.
19. *Ibid*.

20. *Ibid.*
21. *Ibid.*
22. *Ibid.*
23. *Ibid.*
24. *Ibid.*
25. Johnson, Allen and Dumas Malone (eds.), *Dictionary of American Biography*, New York, 1928-1944.
26. Xenophon P. Smith, Librarian, Post Office Department Library, to C. M. Snyder, October 18, 1960.
27. Dr. Mary E. Walker to Kohl and Middleton (n.d.), copy in Poynter mss.
28. Kohl and Middleton to Dr. Mary Walker, October 13, 31, November 1, 1887, Walker mss., Syracuse University.
29. *Toledo Blade*, March 25, 1893; Wonderland program, dated October 21, 1893, Walker mss., Syracuse University.
30. *Oswego Times*, February 22, 1893.
31. *Albany Argus*, November 30, 1895.

Notes to Chapter X

1. *Oswego Times*, January 7, 1881; *Syracuse Courier*, January 8, 1881.
2. C. L. Parker to Dr. Mary Walker, June 28, 1882, Walker mss., Oswego County Historical Society.
3. *Oswego Times*, December 7, 1892.
4. *Ibid.* December 29, 1892.
5. *Ibid.* December 4, 1895.
6. Diary of Aurora Walker Coats, Oswego County Historical Society.
7. Copy in Oswego County Historical Society records.
8. Diary of Aurora Walker Coats.
9. *Oswego Times*, October 19, 1895.
10. Undated newspaper clippings, Walker mss., Syracuse University.
11. W. D. Inslee, "Dr. Mary Walker's Colony of One," *Metropolitan Magazine*, December, 1895.
12. Broadside, published in 1900, Oswego County Historical Society.
13. Mrs. Nicholas to Dr. Mary Walker, July 8, 1913, Sivers mss.; unidentified newspaper clipping, October 1, 1913; *Oswego Times*, December 9, 1913.
14. *Concord Daily People and Patriot*, May 19, 1893; *Nashua Daily Telegraph*, November 11, 1893; *Oswego Times*, October 4, 5, 6, 10, 1893.
15. As told to the author by Charlotte Story Perkinson. See also her "I Knew Her When," *Norfolk Virginian-Pilot* and *Portsmouth Star*, November 22, 1959.
16. *Oswego Times*, January 8, 9, February 1, 2, 8, 1894, *Syracuse Herald*, February 7, 1894; *Syracuse Standard*, February 1, 1894.
17. *Ithaca Journal*, March 2, 1896, quoting *Boston Transcript; Boston Globe*, February 29, March 4, 1896; *Boston Traveller*, March 4, 1896.
18. Henry M. Woods to Mrs. Byron (Vesta) Worden, April 12, 1895,

Sivers mss.; Vashti Walker to Mrs. Byron Worden, July 18, 1895, Sivers mss.

19. Will of Mary Walker of Greenwich, Massachusetts, dated January 12, 1895, Walker mss., Syracuse University; Henry M. Woods to Mrs. Byron Worden, April 28, 1896, Sivers mss.

20. *Springfield Union* (Massachusetts), August 4, September 28, 1897.

Notes to Chapter XI

1. *Oswego Palladium Times*, November 20, 1945 (Centennial Edition).
2. *Oswego Times*, February 22, 1892.
3. This story has appeared many times. For a recent version, see Kay Lucas, *National Parent-Teacher Magazine*, LIV, No. 6 (February, 1960), 19.
4. Hearings before the Committee on the Judiciary, House of Representatives, 62nd Congress, 2nd Session, "Woman Suffrage," by Dr. Mary Walker, February 14, 1912.
5. *Oswego Times*, May 14, 1894.
6. Dr. Joseph B. Ringland, Oswego, N. Y. A slightly different version of the appearance of Mary before the medical academy appears in the *Oswego Palladium*, January 25, 1911.
7. *New York Evening World*, November 23, 1895; *Buffalo Express*, November 25, 1895; *Philadelphia Telegram*, November 23, 1895; *Oswego Palladium*, November 25, 1895, February 24, 1919.
8. *Oswego Palladium*, May 3, 1886.

Notes to Chapter XII

1. Kay Lucas, "Mary Edwards Walker, M.D.,"*National Parent-Teacher Magazine*, LIV, No. 6(February, 1960), 19.
2. *Oswego Palladium*, March 17, 1911.
3. Act to Amend Section 310 of the Public Health Law, Senate Bill No. 437.
4. Dr. Mary E. Walker to the *Oswego Palladium*, May 9, 1910.
5. Mrs. Isabelle Kingsbury Hart, Oswego, N. Y.
6. Marion P. Thomas, "A Visit to Dr. Mary Walker," *The Upstate Monthly*, II, No. 11 (February, 1942), 17-20.
7. Unidentified newspaper clipping, October 1, 1913, Walker mss., Syracuse University.
8. New York State Historical Association, *Proceedings*, XVI, 22, 27; XVII, 15-16.
9. Poynter mss.
10. *Oswego Palladium*, April 11, 1917.
11. *Ibid.* March 30, 1917.
12. Nellie B. Van Slingerland to Dr. Mary Walker, September 12, 1918, Poynter mss.
13. *Syracuse Post Standard*, February 24, 1919.

INDEX

166

Women in America

FROM COLONIAL TIMES TO THE 20TH CENTURY

An Arno Press Collection

Andrews, John B. and W. D. P. Bliss. **History of Women in Trade Unions** (*Report on Conditions of Woman and Child Wage-Earners in the United States,* Vol. X; 61st Congress, 2nd Session, Senate Document No. 645). 1911

Anthony, Susan B. **An Account of the Proceedings on the Trial of Susan B. Anthony, on the Charge of Illegal Voting at the Presidential Election in November, 1872,** and on the Trial of Beverly W. Jones, Edwin T. Marsh and William B. Hall, the Inspectors of Election by Whom her Vote was Received. 1874

The Autobiography of a Happy Woman. 1915

Ayer, Harriet Hubbard. **Harriet Hubbard Ayer's Book:** A Complete and Authentic Treatise on the Laws of Health and Beauty. 1902

Barrett, Kate Waller. **Some Practical Suggestions on the Conduct of a Rescue Home.** *Including* **Life of Dr. Kate Waller Barrett** (Reprinted from *Fifty Years' Work With Girls* by Otto Wilson). [1903]

Bates, Mrs. D. B. **Incidents on Land and Water;** Or, Four Years on the Pacific Coast. 1858

Blumenthal, Walter Hart. **Women Camp Followers of the American Revolution.** 1952

Boothe, Viva B., editor. **Women in the Modern World** (*The Annals of the American Academy of Political and Social Science,* Vol. CXLIII, May 1929). 1929

Bowne, Eliza Southgate. **A Girl's Life Eighty Years Ago:** Selections from the Letters of Eliza Southgate Bowne. 1888

Brooks, Geraldine. **Dames and Daughters of Colonial Days.** 1900

Carola Woerishoffer: Her Life and Work. 1912

Clement, J[esse], editor. **Noble Deeds of American Women;** With Biographical Sketches of Some of the More Prominent. 1851

Crow, Martha Foote. **The American Country Girl.** 1915

De Leon, T[homas] C. **Belles, Beaux and Brains of the 60's.** 1909

de Wolfe, Elsie (Lady Mendl). **After All.** 1935

Dix, Dorothy (Elizabeth Meriwether Gilmer). **How to Win and Hold a Husband.** 1939

Donovan, Frances R. **The Saleslady.** 1929

Donovan, Frances R. **The Schoolma'am.** 1938

Donovan, Frances R. **The Woman Who Waits.** 1920

Eagle, Mary Kavanaugh Oldham, editor. **The Congress of Women,** Held in the Woman's Building, World's Columbian Exposition, Chicago, U.S.A., 1893. 1894

Ellet, Elizabeth F. **The Eminent and Heroic Women of America.** 1873

Ellis, Anne. **The Life of an Ordinary Woman.** 1929

[Farrar, Eliza W. R.] **The Young Lady's Friend.** By a Lady. 1836

Filene, Catherine, editor. **Careers for Women.** 1920

Finley, Ruth E. **The Lady of Godey's:** Sarah Josepha Hale. 1931 **Fragments of Autobiography.** 1974

Frost, John. **Pioneer Mothers of the West;** Or, Daring and Heroic Deeds of American Women. 1869

[Gilman], Charlotte Perkins Stetson. **In This Our World.** 1899

Goldberg, Jacob A. and Rosamond W. Goldberg. **Girls on the City Streets:** A Study of 1400 Cases of Rape. 1935

Grace H. Dodge: Her Life and Work. 1974

Greenbie, Marjorie Barstow. **My Dear Lady:** The Story of Anna Ella Carroll, the "Great Unrecognized Member of Lincoln's Cabinet." 1940

Hourwich, Andria Taylor and Gladys L. Palmer, editors. **I Am a Woman Worker:** A Scrapbook of Autobiographies. 1936

Howe, M[ark] A. De Wolfe. **Memories of a Hostess:** A Chronicle of Friendships Drawn Chiefly from the Diaries of Mrs. James T. Fields. 1922

Irwin, Inez Haynes. **Angels and Amazons:** A Hundred Years of American Women. 1934

Laughlin, Clara E. **The Work-a-Day Girl:** A Study of Some
Present-Day Conditions. 1913

Lewis, Dio. **Our Girls.** 1871

Liberating the Home. 1974

Livermore, Mary A. **The Story of My Life; Or,** The Sunshine
and Shadow of Seventy Years . . . To Which is Added Six
of Her Most Popular Lectures. 1899

Lives to Remember. 1974

Lobsenz, Johanna. **The Older Woman in Industry.** 1929

MacLean, Annie Marion. **Wage-Earning Women.** 1910

Meginness, John F. **Biography of Frances Slocum, the Lost
Sister of Wyoming:** A Complete Narrative of her Captivity of
Wanderings Among the Indians. 1891

Nathan, Maud. **Once Upon a Time and Today.** 1933

[Packard, Elizabeth Parsons Ware]. **Great Disclosure of
Spiritual Wickedness!!** In High Places. With an Appeal to the
Government to Protect the Inalienable Rights of Married Women.
1865

Parsons, Alice Beal. **Woman's Dilemma.** 1926

Parton, James, et al. **Eminent Women of the Age:** Being
Narratives of the Lives and Deeds of the Most Prominent
Women of the Present Generation. 1869

Paton, Lucy Allen. **Elizabeth Cary Agassiz:** A Biography. 1919

Rayne, M[artha] L[ouise]. **What Can a Woman Do; Or,** Her
Position in the Business and Literary World. 1893

Richmond, Mary E. and Fred S. Hall. **A Study of Nine Hundred
and Eighty-Five Widows Known to Certain Charity Organization
Societies in 1910.** 1913

Ross, Ishbel. **Ladies of the Press:** The Story of Women in
Journalism by an Insider. 1936

Sex and Equality. 1974

Snyder, Charles McCool. **Dr. Mary Walker:** The Little Lady in
Pants. 1962

Stow, Mrs. J. W. **Probate Confiscation:** Unjust Laws Which
Govern Woman. 1878

Sumner, Helen L. **History of Women in Industry in the United**

States (*Report on Conditions of Woman and Child Wage-Earners in the United States,* Vol. IX; 61st Congress, 2nd Session, Senate Document No. 645). 1910

[Vorse, Mary H.] **Autobiography of an Elderly Woman.** 1911

Washburn, Charles. **Come into My Parlor:** A Biography of the Aristocratic Everleigh Sisters of Chicago. 1936

Women of Lowell. 1974

Woolson, Abba Gould. **Dress-Reform:** A Series of Lectures Delivered in Boston on Dress as it Affects the Health of Women. 1874

Working Girls of Cincinnati. 1974